Schooling
Young Horses

Schooling
Young Horses

Werner Storl

Translated from the German by
COURTNEY SEARLS-RIDGE
with LOIS M. FEUERLE

Publications, Inc.

Schooling Young Horses is an approved translation of
Die Ausbildung des jungen Pferdes by Werner Storl, published by the
Verlagsbuchhandlung Paul Parey, Berlin and Hamburg, in 1989.

Copyright © 1989 by Verlag Paul Parey, Berlin and Hamburg.
English translation copyright © 1991 by Breakthrough Publications, Inc.

For information address:

Breakthrough Publications, Inc.
Ossining, New York 10562

ISBN 0-914327-36-4
Library of Congress Catalog Card Number: 90-85519

Manufactured in the United States of America

99 98 97 96 95 7 6 5 4 3

Contents

Foreword

This is an excellent book for anyone interested in understanding the true classical approach to dressage. It is well translated and unusually clear and precise in all its descriptions and explanations. As Herr Storl takes pains to point out, it is not a book for a beginner bent on training his or her own young horse. But, fortunately, not many Americans try to do this anymore. If instead a rider comes to dressage after having schooled and shown other types of horses and if he has been able to obtain good private lessons, then the outlook for a well-schooled horse is much better. With the aid of a competent and compatible trainer, he should be able to make good use of Herr Storl's advice as set forth in this book. And, if he is not trying to school his own horse but has put it in the hands of an experienced classical trainer, the book will be of great value in helping him to understand and appreciate the painstaking, slow, and careful development of the horse. So I heartily recommend this book to all serious students of classical dressage.

Long Beach, California   Louise Wilde
December 1990

Preface

Certain basic precepts must be observed to prevent physical and psychological injury to young and green horses when training them as saddle horses for any kind of riding. Unfortunately, as riding has become more and more popular in recent years, there are more improperly and poorly schooled horses than there are those with good, solid training. In many cases, improperly schooled horses are already retired or at the slaughterhouse when a correctly trained horse would just be reaching the pinnacle of its potential.

The schooling of young horses as described in this book is based on traditional classical gymnastic exercises with the goal of preserving and cultivating the horse's innate beauty of movement.

To the benefit of the horse, this book, a combination of traditional advice and years of personal experience, should help many rediscover the often neglected precepts of classical training.

My thanks to my publisher, Paul Parey, for friendly encouragement and support of my work.

Tangstedt, Autumn 1988   Werner Storl

Part One

1

Introduction

With few exceptions, riders are trained in the basics of riding, on more or less appropriate horses, in classes run by stables. After a few years of group lessons, many riders then often wish they owned their own horse. Although in most cases that is too early, many riders are able to fulfill this desire if they are in a financial position to maintain a horse. The reasons for wanting a privately owned horse can be the result of many things: inadequate school horses and the feeling that you will not be able to improve with them; the fallacy that an expensive horse will be easy to ride; the feeling, sometimes valid, that riders who have their own horses see you as second class or otherwise inferior. In truth, there are some stables where student riders are disdained and eventually one tires of the treatment. Of course, the status factor is sometimes a motivator as well.

In any case, many riders buy their first horse much too early. Worse still, they buy the *wrong* horse. Often, the first horse has already been spoiled by poor training and consequently ends up at the slaughterhouse too soon. Unfortunately, many riders know precious little about the basics of caring for and schooling young horses. Helplessly, they ask everyone for advice and quick cures, but do not bother to seek out the experts. I have often observed the development of such young horses and in most cases they end up ruined and poorly trained.

This book addresses riders considering acquiring an unschooled (green) horse. It also contains advice and help for those of you who have already taken that first step.

When are you ready for your own horse?

The time has come to acquire your own horse when you have good mastery of the skills required for the lowest level dressage tests. The emphasis is on the word "good." In my opinion, it takes a rider in a weekly class *at least* five years to reach this level. To be ready for your own horse sooner, you would need excellent private lessons on a good school horse at least twice a week for about two or three years.

Obviously, the financial side of keeping your own horse must also be carefully considered. Most riders think only about purchase price and stable costs, but there are several other expenses to consider: blacksmithing, veterinary care (worming and vaccinations), insurance, and riding lessons.

There is yet another question the prospective horse owner should ask: Do I really have the time for my own horse? A horse is not a piece of sports equipment or a means of transportation that you can use when convenient and let sit when you are too busy. A horse requires significant *daily* exercise, on Christmas Eve, Christmas Day, and the day after Christmas — when the ground is icy and during snow storms — whether you feel like it or not, no matter how much you have to do at the office. This time commitment is something that prospective horse owners never accurately predict. If you are considering buying your own horse, ask your riding instructor for advice first.

How to find the right horse

Before beginning this section, let me make one thing very clear: a bronze medal for riding and the equestrian skills necessary to achieve this award are no indication that you are ready to acquire a *young*, just broken, worse yet, green horse. The schooling of young horses belongs in the hands of experienced equestrians, and there are fewer of them around than one might expect.

For most riders the first horse is a school horse they fell in love with at the riding school. Their reasons for buying him are that he is "sweet," behaves well cross-country, and they do all right on him in dressage work in the indoor riding arena with side reins or martingale. These school horse characteristics are reason enough for most riders to buy and, if they are not interested in anything more than hacking, these may be acceptable.

On the other hand, some riders are attracted to buying a *difficult* horse, one that gives other riders in the class a hard time, but which performs well with the help of a draw rein. The stable owner, of course, is interested in the sale of such a horse and will advise you to buy.

Unfortunately, the health of the horse is often not given enough consideration. As important as it is to buy a healthy horse, few school riders can evaluate whether or not a horse is really sound, is free in the back, is a pacer, or has a tendency toward paddling, winging, or forging, or has arthritis, for instance. In any case, you should ask the opinion of an objective experienced rider, and perhaps that of a veterinarian. If your main consideration is price, you are bound to be disappointed. Stallions, thoroughbreds, and even half-bred horses do not belong in the hands of someone who has just outgrown riding school. The same is true of young, green, or newly broken horses. Although one should not generalize when it comes to riding, one point must be absolutely clear. Stay away from trotters; you cannot re-train them for dressage. The canter will always be deficient and be a four-beat gait.

Most riders change stables after buying their first horse. They have reached their goal, and now they want to move up to a private stable. It is here that disappointment quickly sets in when they discover they can't handle the horse, especially because they thought they no longer needed an instructor. From the next teacher, they later hear about the problems, shortcomings, and flaws of their newly acquired horse. Usually these are that he has a thick lower neck, a lack of impulsion, a lateral walk, no rhythm, poor gaits, tongue problems, major flexion flaws, and signs of wear and tear on the forelegs.

Astonished, the new horse owner is now made aware of problems he has never heard of before, and all this time he thought he was an experienced rider. In the course of the next few weeks, he will finally realize that he has bought the wrong horse. But he will keep it because he loves it. This is the end of his development as a rider; the dream of being a dressage competitor is over.

This is what usually happens when someone buys the first horse. Luckily, there are some exceptions. More often than one would think, however, because of an eternal know-it-all attitude even the *second* horse is bought without asking expert advice. But the dreamers who won't listen to reason will never attain the dream of even lower level dressage.

Now let's finally discuss the right way to acquire a horse. Every experienced riding instructor knows when a student is ready for the move to a private horse. Ask your trainer to scout around for an appropriate horse for you. Your instructor will know your strengths and weaknesses, as well as your physical and emotional predispositions, and will be able to help find the horse that is right for you. Most appropriate would be a horse that is not too young (seven to ten years old), usually trained for elementary dressage. It must be healthy, keen, and have a flawless disposition. When you think you have found a suitable horse, then follow these steps:

- Let someone ride the horse in your presence;
- Let your riding instructor test ride the horse;
- Ride the horse yourself to see if it feels comfortable and is easy to manage;
- Make sure you like the horse;
- Be sure the horse moves all four legs flawlessly.

Obviously, your riding instructor should check for irregularity of gaits, any wounds or scars, or any problems with the legs such as windpuffs and bowed tendons. You should also observe how the horse behaves in the stall to see if it cribs or weaves.

It goes without saying that the person brought along to evaluate the horse must truly know horses in order to be able to judge the character, and also be familiar with faults that might affect the performance of the horse. Finally, don't decide to buy until all of these tests and observations have been made, and even then, ask a trusted vet to examine the horse.

The following flaws are considered *major faults* or faults that legally constitute breach of warranty in Germany: mucous discharge, respiratory problems, roaring, chronic eye inflammation, and cribbing.

Your intended purpose will, of course, also have a lot to do with the choice of a horse. Do you want a horse for hacking and long-distance riding, as a school horse to continue to learn dressage, or as a jumper and event horse? It should be emphasized here again that it will still be several years before a rider coming from group lessons will be good enough to think about show-jumping competitions or events.

When looking for your own horse there are still other factors to keep in mind, such as age, size, level of training, and disposition. Nervous riders, for instance, belong with calm, lazy horses, and quiet riders belong with sensitive, keen horses. Horses that move on the forehand belong with riders who know how to engage the hindquarters. Obviously, a person who weighs a lot needs a heavy horse with strong enough bone structure and good muscle structure.

When buying a horse, don't forget that no matter how good and well-trained the horse is, if it is ridden by a weak rider, it won't be a good horse for long. The best advice is to look for a mediocre used horse and invest the rest of your available funds in good lessons rather than buying an expensive horse and neglecting instruction.

- *Remember*: A good rider gets better performance from an average horse than a poor rider gets from a great horse.

Because we can't expect a lot of experience from a rider just out of group lessons, it is extremely important to ask a trustworthy teacher to help choose your first horse. It is here that the possibilities for further growth as an equestrian begin.

Many more pages could be written about the right horse, but it's time to get to the subject of this book, as the title says, and talk about *young* horses.

Choosing and buying a young horse

If you are buying a young horse with the intention of schooling it yourself, you should have at least mastered elementary dressage. Even then, you should have an experienced rider supervise training.

Before buying a young horse, you must know what to look for. Only then will you be able to judge a horse. It is not possible here to get into the larger science of theory of motion and understanding fundamental quality of horses. However, I strongly advise all potential buyers to learn about these areas before buying, and I recommend the following books: Heling, Dr. 1964: *Das Vollendete Pferd*. Frankfurt/M: DLG Verlag. Knopfhart, A. 1987: *Beurteilung und Auswahl von Reitpferden*. 4th ed. Berlin and Hamburg: Paul Parey.*

These books contain the knowledge necessary to buy a horse and explain technical terms and concepts that a horseowner must know,

* [Regarding German books mentioned within the text, I have left titles in German. Although it is not common practice to translate book titles in translations (because it makes it nearly impossible for an interested reader to track down the original), I have translated the bibliography at the end of the book. — Trans.]

such as "square horse," "rectangular horse," well-balanced, inside, outside, frame, potential, good through the jowl, pedigree, for example.

There are so many factors to consider when buying a horse that you cannot spend too much time with the literature. Unfortunately, many riders do not do this before buying, but, rather, after. Again and again you see horses that are not appropriate as riding horses and even less appropriate to be trained for dressage. Over and over I hear, "If I had only known all that before." How could a school rider, even if he has been taking group lessons for years, know enough about conformation, pace, impulsion, character, temperament, or a horse's ability to be ridden? Hackneyed jargon such as the horse engages, accepts the bit, carries itself, arches its neck on the aids, sounds good and might impress a beginner or some school riders, but is no indication of knowledge. Few know what they're talking about.

The most important factors to look for have already been addressed in the section, "How to find the right horse." Now I would like to point out a few things to keep in mind when buying a *young* horse.

Unbroken or green broke

Whether to buy a horse that is already broken is a difficult decision to make. A broken horse is obviously easier to evaluate than one that is not, because you can observe it being ridden and better judge its action, how it engages its hindquarters, and the manner in which it moves in general. You can also test ride the horse yourself, because often an experienced rider feels more than he sees. But if you buy a horse that is already broken, there is some danger that it has been incorrectly broken and already partially spoiled.

A horse that has not been broken must be trained by a true expert, because the foundation for its entire development is laid during the first few days and weeks of schooling. It's usually worse to buy an incorrectly broken horse than a horse that has never been backed.

Willingness to go forward.

This is another important guideline to go by when evaluating a young horse. It is a rare quality and a gift of nature. All of the horse's power must come from its *hindquarters,* and its *strike-off* should be elevated. Keep in mind that physical flaws are easier to correct than *character flaws.* If the *eye* is the mirror of the human soul, this is also true for horses. In other words, watch for ambling paces, paddling or winging, and other *pace irregularities.* Also take a look at the lower neck, check for jaw yielding and hanging tongue. Observe the horse in the stable and look for crib biting, weaving, and kicking against the walls of the stall. Perhaps you can also find out something about the horse from the stable personnel or blacksmith. No matter what, you should not neglect the advice of an experienced rider who knows how to evaluate young horses.

- *Remember:* Evaluate the horse objectively, but try not to be over critical. Always judge the *whole* horse. It must have personality. You must like it.

Again, it should be emphasized that young or unbroken horses do not belong in the hands of beginners. A bronze medal or lowest level dressage prizes do not qualify you to be a trainer of young horses; only the really experienced rider or professional is capable of that.

- *Remember:* A young horse, whether unbroken or green broke, does not belong in the hands of a beginner.

In addition, every rider who buys a young horse should be aware of the fact that it takes about two years to school a young horse to the lowest level. None of the popular quick methods or shortcuts work, rather they impede development of the horse. Furthermore, don't forget that basic schooling is also important and absolutely necessary for horses that are just for hacking or leisure horses, because particularly in leisure riding, serious accidents occur that are often the result of inadequately trained horse and rider.

Caution is also advised with horses that are already broken and with those being offered as lowest level trained. Often (unfortunately more than one thinks) these horses have been trained by riders who have not much more to offer than courage and overconfidence. Sales stables are often connected with these. Find out exactly who broke or trained the horse you want to buy. What good is a horse who performs beautiful figures or even flying change of lead under an accomplished rider to a rider who is barely lowest level himself? Only the basic paces and suppleness are important. Try to be critical of all other showing off tactics. I have known several riders who have paid enormous sums of money for horses that had placed at medium dressage but in the years that followed never even placed at the lowest level. The desire to be known often plays a large role when buying a horse.

- *Remember:* When buying a horse, rule out all thoughts of personal prestige.

2

The way to school

Classic equitation has developed principles, some of which date from the fifth and fourth centuries B.C. and which can still be read in Xenophon's equestrian literature (*The Art of Horsemanship and The Cavalry Commander*).

The importance of the classic tenets of riding has also been confirmed again and again throughout the centuries, and many older riders learned the basics of horsemanship from the almost legendary Germany Army Regulation Handbook (HDv. 12 published in 1912, revised in 1926 and 1937). In fact, today's guidelines for basic schooling are still based on these publications. Whenever new methods of basic schooling have been attempted over the years, the new ways have been found to be ineffective. The 1984 Olympic Games in Los Angeles proved once again that classic schooling, as previously implemented at the Hannover Cavalry Academy, still works today; this is true for both rider and horse. So far, Americans have been most successful in Olympic jumping and three-day eventing with their rediscovery of these classic tenets.

Training phases

The progress of a horse that has been recently been broken in, a remount, to a schooled saddle horse follows these phases:

1. familiarization,
2. work on the longe,

3. finding balance under a rider working straight lines,
4. developing impulsion,
5. lateral work,
6. cavaletti work,
7. developing collection.

*   *Remember*: A bad beginning can never be brought to a good end.

Familiarization

Many riders do not take this first phase of training seriously enough, although it forms the entire basis for how the horse will react to people. The horse must not only adjust completely to a new stable environment, but also to its new owner and different feeding habits, not to mention bridle, saddle, and longe. Changes in feeding should be initiated very cautiously. In general, a young horse should be given plenty of time to inspect his new home and get used to new smells. He also has to work out new stable noises. If you board your horse, it is advantageous to allow the stable hand to feed it and later help train it, because the horse needs a person who is both a reference person and authority figure. The smell and familiar appearance of this person are very important in this respect.

From the very first day, the familiarization phase and the training phase overlap. Lifting the legs daily (in the correct order: front left, back left, front right, back right) is just as important as the daily grooming routine. When grooming, it is very important to be gentle and use soft brushes and cloth around the head. This is also the time to begin with the snaffle, but be careful that the bit does not hit the teeth hard. Great care must be given to fitting the bridle. Under no circumstances must the buckle of the nose band be allowed to push against the jaw bone. All tasks should be carried out calmly, with no sudden hand or arm movements.

First saddling

The horse should be allowed to sniff and look at the saddle pad and saddle for several days before the first time it is put on his back. The first time should be in a familiar place, perhaps in the horse's stall. While an assistant speaks to the horse and gives it little pieces of bread or carrots, someone else lays the saddle *pad* on the horse. Once the horse is used to it, lay the *saddle* on him without stirrups and girth at first. Take your time for this procedure. It does not all have to happen in one day.

Once the horse has accepted the saddle, add the girth, but still without stirrups. This is the time to bridle the horse and lead it to the arena. If your horse wants to arch its back, take off, or throw itself to the ground when it is girthed or during the first few steps under the saddle, it should not be allowed to hurt itself. This is why we avoid the hard floor of the stable aisle, go to the arena, and use a longe line for added safety.

After putting on the saddle and loose girth very carefully and calmly, lead the horse a few steps, remove the saddle, and praise the horse. This first excursion with loose girth, following grooming, should be all that is on the agenda for the day. Your horse needs the time and opportunity to process this new experience; don't be tempted to do too much at once. The next day, repeat the procedure and take the horse for a slightly longer walk, carefully tightening the girth.

Now the time has come to teach starting on track and coming to a halt. Take the reins from the neck, leading as always with the right hand and holding the ends of the reins in the left. Use the commands "walk on" and "halt" to teach the horse his first lessons in hand.

Over and over again one hears about riders who know about these things, but who do not pay attention to them. They think it is ridiculous and much too slow to train using such an old-fashioned method. Using drastic rodeo methods, they show an amazed audience tricks. Their horses break away and get tangled up in trailing longeing lines, or they rear and go over backward attempting to rid themselves of the unfamiliar saddle.

You don't have to have studied animal behavior to grasp that this kind of treatment may ruin the horse for the rest of its life; saddlephobia (also known as cold-back), girthphobia, rearing, and other bad behavior are just a few of the disastrous consequences. When girthing, the rule is always to tighten the girth a little and lead the horse a few steps in between before tightening it again. In this breaking phase of training there are several other important things to pay attention to.

Saddle pads

As I mentioned when discussing saddling for the first time, the horse should be allowed to get used to the pad first before the saddle is introduced. Saddle pads or blankets should be made of wool and should be put on the horse's back several times before the first saddling. The saddle is much more pleasant over a non-irritating, folded wool pad than on a thin linen or polyester blanket. Later, the pad or blanket also softens the pressure of the weight of a rider. If you use wool blankets, they should always be folded with the folds facing the front and right (the left side is the near side). Don't forget to adjust the saddle pad. Finally, when washing blankets and felts it is very important to rinse carefully. The combination of detergent residue and horse perspiration can cause serious skin damage.

Tying

The first time a horse is tethered, make a loop out of thin twine between the tether ring and the lead shank so that if the horse pulls on it, it will rip quickly with little resistance. If tied incorrectly, there is danger that the horse will get into the habit of straining the ties and ripping its halter and shank. This often causes horses to stumble and have accidents. Be particularly careful when tying horses that already have acquired the bad habit of throwing themselves over backward. I have seen more than one severed finger that got caught in the cross ties. So the word "handling" refers not only to the horse, but also to the safety of the trainer who is in much more danger working with young horses than with schooled and well-behaved horses.

Feeding

When working with young horses—whether on the longe or in the saddle—be careful not to overfeed and get the horse too hot. Frisky bucking and jumping are not particularly helpful in training and always carry with them the danger of tendon and joint injury. It will be difficult to find a rider willing to sit on such a "hot horse." The best time to work with young horses is early in the morning when the riding arena is empty. Experience also shows that horses are calmer in the morning hours.

This is a good place to talk a bit about giving treats. Praise and reprimand, i.e., reward and punishment, are integral when training horses. But punishment does not necessarily mean whipping. With young horses most praise and reprimand is done with voice. If we want to give a horse special praise, it should be in the form of a small piece of bread or carrot, *never sugar*. Sugar on a horse's lips sometimes makes the horse lick the bit or manger causing the horse to hang his tongue and possibly leading to sucking wind. You should really only give treats as a reward — not imprudently out of misplaced love of animals; this makes many horses rebellious and disobedient.

Because the words "manners" and "obedience" come up all the time when talking about training young horses, let me mention a few basics here. All problems and difficulties that appear later in training are the result of poor or incorrect basic training during the first few weeks and months. Upbringing plays a significant role in this. How many horses do you see every day that:

- swell themselves up or try to bite the rider while being saddled,
- are unruly while being bridled,
- will not stand still while being mounted,
- will not follow commands on the longe,
- will not keep a steady pace with loose reins or stay on track,
- want to gallop or jump over every ground rail?

This list could go on forever, but in every case we are talking about ill-mannered horses. So, just as it is a pleasure to be around well-mannered people, it is fun to work with well-mannered horses. Please understand that we do not want a broken creature, insensitive or unspirited, but rather an animal that will be a partner, spirited in relation to his age, with personality, character and willingness to work pleasantly. With this in mind, let's move on to longe work.

3

Work on the longe

Longeing has nothing to do with letting a horse run around or be chased around on a rein with a whip and yelled at loudly. Longeing must be learned, just as riding must be learned. Unfortunately, correct longeing is seldom taught today — and there are few riders who are willing to take classes in longeing and the theory behind it, much less pay to do so. Arrogance and lack of understanding of the fundamentals of riding are the reasons, and as a result many horses are spoiled by incompetent work on the longe.

The longe is where real schooling begins, because it is here that the horse learns about aids for the first time and about the basics of obedience. In addition, the horse has to learn a few basic lessons such as:

* to walk on a circle,
* to become accustomed to spoken commands and to understand the concepts underlying the commands,
* to be familiar with a whip and a martingale,
* basic paces,
* to understand reward and correction,
* to halt on the circle,
* suppleness,
* to be driven forward.

None of these lessons or phases of longeing work stands alone, but rather they all overlap and complement each other.

At any rate, you can see that we are talking about a tremendous learning assignment, and perhaps you already realize that longeing is something very different than you may have thought. The horse will not be ready to move on to further training or be backed until these goals have been reached. It is absolutely necessary that an experienced longe trainer supervise this developmental phase of the horse in order to spot mistakes earlier on and correct them.

When to start the first work on a longe

An old adage says that every horse should spend the summer of its third year turned out in the field — bones, tendons, and joints of young-sters are delicate and can be easily injured if longe work starts too early. So training should begin in the fall of the third year.

After leading the horse in hand around the ring several times, begin longeing work on a large circle. For the first few days, an assistant will be needed to lead the horse around the circle while the trainer stands in the center holding the longe rein.

The trainer always remains in the middle of the circle while the assistant stays directly behind the longe guiding the horse around the large circle from behind, preferably on the left-hand side first. Do not use a whip in the beginning. When the horse has learned to follow the curve of the circle, the assistant may move toward the center away from the horse, but should at first still be directly behind the longe. When far enough away from the horse, the assistant positions himself slightly behind the longe and holds the longeing whip in his outer hand pointing the tip toward the horse's hock. To drive the horse forward, he takes the whip behind the horse and swings the lash from behind against the hock trying to get by at first with a "driving posture."

Before using the whip the first time you should get the horse used to it by patting him on the back and haunches with the folded whip, so that he will not be afraid of it. Halting, which has already been prac-ticed leading on the hand, is facilitated first by the assistant holding the halter.

All of this should take place in a calm and relaxed manner always being careful not to try too much at a time. For the first day it is enough to work at walk on the left rein with a few additional rounds at trot. Don't forget reward and correction with small pieces of bread, always given while the horse is standing on the circle; the horse should never be brought to the center of the circle.

The first longe work lays the basis for obedience, so the trainer must issue all commands to the horse in an audible voice. The horse understands not what you say but rather how you say it. With a firm tone of the voice issue the commands: Waaalk-on, tr-aaat, haaalt, and the short command, canter.

Let me say a few words here about the longeing ring and equipment. Of course, the ideal is a circle set aside especially for longeing, such as the longeing rings found in many arenas in Germany. The advantage is that the boundaries are marked to give the horse guidelines. Another advantage of a longeing ring is that the floor is properly cared for and free of grooves. When there is no longeing ring available, owners of young horses will always have problems with the other riders in the stable over the use of inside and outside areas. If this is the case, and also with the best interest of your horse in mind, you should try to find times of the day when there are fewer riders around. You can set up bales of hay or wings as boundaries for longeing in an outside arena.

Equipment

The required equipment consists of:

- longeing cavesson,
- longeing surcingle,
- longe line usually made of nylon and twenty-five feet long,
- longeing whip (not too heavy),
- two side reins,
- bandages or brushing boots.

The ideal longeing cavesson fits snugly and does not disturb the horse's mouth in any way. If there is no cavesson available, use a snaffle. To do this, hook the longe line to the inside snaffle ring. Because there is a risk that the bit might be pulled inward, you should also buckle the halter to the longe line.

With horses that lean to the outside, the longeing rein should be run through the inside snaffle ring, drawn over the poll, and snapped in the outside snaffle ring. This operation is, however, fairly difficult and requires a sensitive hand. A strap hooked into both sides of the snaffle rings will also prevent the bit from being pulled through the mouth.

The lash of the longeing whip must be long enough to reach the horse from the center of the circle, but it should not be too heavy.

Both side reins are buckled sideways to the surcingle and snaffle ring. Let's stay with the side reins for a while. When the horse is first getting used to the longe he should be led *without* side reins. Later, both sides are attached — but never when walking. Longeing lessons — as riding lessons later — must begin with loose, or long, reins so that the horse can stretch completely forward and downward. This loosening up or stretching phase at the beginning of each lesson is very important; side reins would make it impossible to lengthen the topline. In trot and canter, side reins are attached in such a way that the horse's noseline is slightly but definitely in front of the vertical. Toward the end of the longeing lesson you should unbuckle the side reins again so that the horse can stretch and relax again at walk.

The first longeing should begin before the horse is used to the saddle; subsequent longeing work will always be with the horse saddled and bridled. When longeing young horses the stirrups should always be pulled up and hooked so that they do not dangle around irritating the horse during the lesson. Later, in preparation for the first backing and to get the horse used to stirrups, you can longe with the stirrups down. However, I strongly recommend that you first walk the horse with dangling stirrups. With strong horses that have a tendency to arch, romp, and rear, it is best not to longe them at this stage with dangling stirrups because of the danger that if the horse falls he will get caught up in the stirrups.

Sometimes other aids are used in longeing work: side reins buckled over the back, chambon, running reins, or double longeing lines. Some trainers with years of experience longeing young horses have developed their own methods, but leave this to the real experts. For the novice trainer reading this book, classical longeing — proven effective over and over again through the years — is recommended.

In several days, when the horse seems accustomed to the circular arc and you no longer require assistance, real work on the longe begins. Stand exactly in the middle of the circle and pivot — in other words, do not run in a little circle with the horse. Your outside shoulder is turned slightly toward the horse, the inside shoulder pulled slightly back. The longe is held — including the coiled excess line — in the inside hand at the level of the horse's mouth (about breast height), the whip is in the outside hand. We use the expressions "inside and outside" when referring to longeing just as in riding, so that the rider turns as if he were sitting on the horse. The longeing rein should never hang down or skirt the ground.

Point the whip at the horse's hock. If you wish to increase drive, bring the lash along behind the horse, maybe even touching the hock. If the horse falls in toward the center of the circle, position the whip at the horse's shoulder and operate toward the outside (from top to bottom). Another way to keep the horse out on the circle is with a vibrating motion of the longe. At first though, voice is the primary aid in longe work and only one person should work with the horse so that the animal gets used to the familiar voice and habits of this person. At the beginning and end of a lesson as well as when changing hands, the trainer should always go to the horse and praise it; the horse should never be brought to the trainer. When working on the longe, the horse should always be framed — as when riding — between the leading hand and the driving whip, which substitutes for leg at this stage (Figure 1).

Young horses are easily frightened and often their movements are unpredictable, so the whip should never leave your hand or be placed on the ground. Tuck it under your arm when it is not in use.

Work always begins on the left rein, because most horses will comply on this side, and always begin lessons at a walk. Avoid beginning lessons by letting the horse romp or canter right away, which could result in injuries to tendons and joints. The articular capsules, dry from standing, need time to lubricate and limber up. The muscles also need to be worked at walk first to stimulate circulation of blood thereby warming them. Athletes warm up before working out and we should insist our horses do the same.

It is normal for young horses to frolic, but this should not be forced or encouraged and under no circumstances should longe work begin with romping. If a horse insists on gamboling continuously as work increases, check to make sure that he is not being overfed.

If your horse offers a canter and starts up correctly then you should give him full play. However, it is extremely important to let the longe out all the way in canter so that the horse has the whole circle on which to canter. Cantering on a small circle will most certainly result in leg injuries later.

As mentioned before, the horse should always go without side reins at walk so that it can stretch its head forward and downward. Once this is achieved, it is time to fit the tack. The inside rein is fitted somewhat

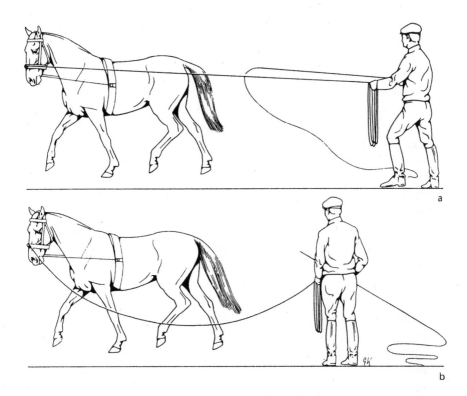

a

b

Figure 1. Framed between whip and longe. (a) Correct.
(b) Incorrect; the horse is not framed and the longe is hanging loose.
(Reprinted from Müseler, 1981.)

tighter than the outside rein so that the horse bends slightly toward the
inside. The noseline must always be in front of the vertical so that the
horse can stretch into the outside rein.

The right side requires tremendous patience and skill in the beginning because it often causes problems. In the beginning, you may need
an assistant who, as in the first longeing lesson, runs alongside the
horse's head, later moving more toward the center of the circle, and
taking over the whip. Much change of hand and praise are necessary at
this stage. Remember to refit the side reins when changing hands.

The first longe lessons should last about twenty minutes. Later this
can be increased to thirty minutes. Change hands every five minutes,
working the more difficult side harder. Also work hard on halting using

a voice command; do not allow the horse to push inward or bring his head in. In trot the horse should find a regular, relaxed tempo and let himself be driven.

Once the horse has mastered a walk and trot on the longe, you can begin with the canter. To do this, bring the trotting horse slightly into the circle to increase the inside curve. Let the longe out again immediately, at the same time using the whip to drive and the voice command to canter. Using these aids, most horses will naturally canter on the correct foot. If the horse returns on its own to a trot, do not chase it into a canter immediately, but give it a chance to find its rhythm and position in trot, and then try again with the canter. In the transition from canter to trot, use a short longe line against the stride and encourage the horse with words.

A horse that has been well-trained on the longe will later respond almost without voice commands, just with the longe and hint of the whip; even tempo changes can be executed in this manner.

There should be time at the end of every longe lesson for free walk without side reins to allow uninhibited stretching forward and downward. Real work at walk should never take place with a tightly reined horse, because rather than encouraging the pace this will inhibit it.

The goals of longe work

The horse should:

- move forward in all paces, keeping on the circle, and halting on command on the circle;
- move forward unconstrainedly, calmly, and smoothly in all paces, neither holding back nor charging ahead;
- extend the neck and pull the reins downward and forward;
- have reached a level of suppleness appropriate for its development.

Work on the longe must always last long enough for the horse to be driven forward with a long neck and swinging tail, i.e., not rushing ahead. But longeing does not mean — particularly later when concluding with work in the saddle — tiring the horse. The horse should only be getting rid of excess energy and boisterousness.

Once the objective has been learned, the time has come to back the horse for the first time, assuming that the last phase of longeing has been with a saddle.

As mentioned earlier, if a three-year old has spent the summer in the field, longe work should begin in the fall, and within a few weeks the horse can be prepared for work with a rider.

- *Remember*: All longe work should be carried out with resolve, at the same time remaining absolutely calm and patient.

4

Lessons under saddle

Introduction

Keep in mind that the following chapter deals with training horses, not riders. I have already explained what prerequisites and skills the rider or trainer of young horses should bring to the task. Our present training program is based on decades, sometimes centuries, of experience and has been developed over the years by famous riders and trainers. If you compare guidelines for training young horses in 1882 or 1912 to those of today, you will see that there are no basic differences. The main difference is simply that the earlier guidelines were much more detailed and comprehensive. In the old books you will find, for example, instructions for riding on ice and mud, swimming with horses, climbing, and riding with a lead horse and a reserve horse.

The importance that was previously assigned to schooling and trainers is evident from the fact that at the turn of the nineteenth century, riding instructors employed by estate owners and universities were on a level with professors. (Seuning, W. 1965: *Reitergedanken am langen Zügel*. Heidenheim: Erich Hoffmann.)

Young horses used to be called remounts. A *young* remount referred to a horse in the first year of training, an *older* remount referred to a horse in the second year of training. The literature indicates that basic training required about two years. No matter how pedantic and boring these first two years seem, they are the foundation for everything else. Any fault that shows up later is the result of something that has not been properly dealt with in this first stage. This period, no matter how long it takes, is never wasted. The biggest mistake during this period is to ask too much too soon, not only physically, but psychologically as well.

Horses can be early bloomers or late bloomers, lazy or energetic, calm or high-strung. An experienced trainer will individually structure lessons and the amount of work to fit each horse. Calmness, patience, and moderate expectations are absolutely necessary. Be happy with small successes.

A basic training plan, giving careful consideration to individual strengths and weaknesses, is necessary for the long run, but should never be adhered to too strictly.

* *Remember*: Do not train young horses unless you have
  infinite patience.

The training plan

The goal of training with a rider is to use gymnastic exercises to develop the horse's natural gaits. You must always take into consideration the stage of physical development and never overtax the horse psychologically.

First stage - Loosening work and drive

* Finding its balance under the rider.
* Developing rhythm and drive.
* Suppleness.
* Bending work using inside aids.
* Putting the horse to the aids.
* Riding outdoors.

Second stage - Straightening out and impulsion

* Introducing the outside aids and longitudinal bending of the spine.
* Lengthening and shortening.
* Halts.
* Cantering.

Third phase - Collection and Elevation

* Improving contact.

- Developing supportive power in the hindquarters.
- Raising the forehand by lowering the hindquarters.
- Riding in flexion, developing shoulder in.

Fourth Phase — Working with a curb bit

The last phase of training involves advanced work with a curb bit.

This plan of training has a logical basis. It would be difficult, however, to express the process in an absolute or concrete formula, because each stage evolves from the previous one. The main ingredients are the rider's experience and intuition. Each principal of dressage is a useful tool. None is an end in itself, be it a lesson in loosening, bending, or collecting. For this reason, specific exercises and lessons are not listed for each stage of this training schedule.

In general, the training schedule is based on two concepts; balance and gymnastics. The concept of *balance* (or center of gravity) is the main point of consideration throughout the discourse which follows, so it is not discussed in detail here. With regard to *gymnastics*, while in training, in addition to familiarization and obedience, a young horse must also learn specific positions and master certain lessons. To achieve this the entire locomotor system, including muscles, tendons, joints, and heart and the circulatory system, must be developed, strengthened, and empowered. Muscles can be built up only by working them — the right work builds the right muscles, the wrong work builds the wrong muscles. Dressage in this sense means nothing but gymnastics, whereby both sides of the horse, left and right, must be developed *equally*.

- *Remember*:   Correct riding renders a horse beautiful;
  incorrect riding renders a horse ugly.

First backing and riding

The horse has already had some preparation for the first backing during previous longe work with a saddle. In addition, the rider has been lifted up occasionally to lie across the saddle. The horse must get used to the height and size of a rider. It is not the unaccustomed weight of the rider on the horse's back as much as the fearful size of a rider that frightens the horse and makes it want to run away. The first backing should proceed with great patience and encouragement to the horse. Yelling or hitting will only increase the horse's fear.

Ideally, the first backing should follow longeing in the arena. A lightweight rider is preferable to a heavier rider. With the rider mounted the horse should be led for a few minutes or a few paces with gentle continuous verbal encouragement. Then the rider should dismount immediately and praise the horse. Follow the same procedure a little longer the next day, and in the days that follow the horse should be walked on the longe, perhaps with a few occasional trots, while the rider sits passively in the saddle — no back, leg off, loose reins.

Within several days the horse will be far enough along for free riding to begin. At first, it will be necessary to have an assistant help when mounting and to run alongside the horse. Soon the rider will be able to sit with stirrups. Sometimes it is advisable to use a lead horse walking beside the horse being trained. In this case, the young horse is always in the outside lane (see Figure 2).

Finding balance riding straight lines

The first thing a young horse must now do is get used to the weight of the rider and learn how to balance with the rider — it has to relearn how to walk. This is only possible when riding at first in a straight line, where possible, only in a walk, keeping in mind the following:

- Sit absolutely still;
- Use no back muscle;
- Press thighs lightly against the horse but remain passive;
- Maintain slight contact to both hands but do not use rein aids;
- Do not use spurs;
- Encourage the horse verbally and maybe even with a small whip at the horse's shoulder;
- Keep curves to a minimum.

If your horse wants to trot or gallop, try to restrain him using as little rein guidance as possible. Do not use hard reins to bring him to a halt, because he is not yet familiar with the reins as an aid to halt. Pull in slowly and reinforce this with voice commands, which your horse knows from longe work. Under no circumstances should you fall off

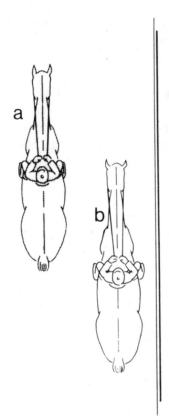

Figure 2. (a) Lead horse.
(b) Young horse.

your horse in this first phase because the horse would be quick to discover what fun it is to remove a rider from his back in this way.

During the first days and weeks the horse should never be over-worked. Work your horse on the longe first and then ride it for only a few minutes, extending the time up to twenty minutes or so depending on the stamina and temperament of the horse. Never work a horse to the point of exhaustion. Many horses are never given enough time to balance out as youngsters. Often they are whipped into shape, to use an expression. These are the horses who never really take the reins later on. After several days, once the horse has found his center of gravity fairly well, it is time to begin training at walk with loose reins and basic (or natural) trot with light contact.

* *Remember:* Be very generous with praise.

Walking with loose reins (free walk)

During the first few days of backing, a young horse will tense, lift its head, tuck its tail under, and push away with a tight back. So the first goal of training must be to relax the horse, allowing full neck extension and lengthening the horse from front to back. At walk with loose (hanging) reins the horse should be extending his head and neck forward and downward. This posture allows a horse to carry the rider with the neck and back ligaments, relaxing the back muscles and allowing for good circulation. A horse must be relaxed and the muscles must be well-supplied with blood before it is ready for work. For example, if you put a heavy load on the back of a person with normal (straight) posture, he will bend forward and carry the weight on a curved back (like a bridge), stretching head and neck forward and downward. In this way the neck and head help carry the load.

A horse must take on exactly the same posture in order to carry the unaccustomed weight of a rider. But a horse can only stretch forward and downward if it is not restrained by the reins. The reins must hang loosely, and your hands must leave the horse's mouth alone.

If you speak constantly to the horse, pat him, and run your hands through his mane, the horse will soon trust you enough to stretch out. It is very important that the horse should discover the first gentle contact with the bit deep in the mouth while remaining in this forward and downward position. This is the only posture that strengthens the horse's back.

If the horse does not lengthen in spite of completely loose reins, than carefully take up both reins equally, and gently exert slight, even pressure on the horse's mouth until you sense that the horse is resisting by pulling forward and downward. At that moment, let up on the rein and seek contact with the horse's mouth. Of course, this is also the moment for praise and patting.

The nodding movement of a horse at walk is of utmost importance for the development of neck and back muscles and it should never be inhibited by the rider's hand. As a matter of fact, it is not only for muscle development and balance that we work with completely loose reins at walk; there is also a great risk that if the bit is taken too early in a walk, it can disturb the sequence of gait and the horse will pace. Many horses are inadvertently taught a lateral walk during the beginning stages of training.

A calm supple seat with lightly applied leg is a prerequisite for this first important phase of breaking a horse.

Natural trot with light contact

You must always strive to begin saddle work at walk even if you have been working with the longe beforehand. Every riding lesson begins at walk, because the young horse relaxes most quickly at walk with loose reins. Another reason to begin at walk is described in the chapter dealing with work on the longe in the discussion on lubrication of the articular capsules.

One exception to this rule is in winter when the arena is very cold. Then, after one or two circles at walk, you should begin with a warm-up trot to keep your horse from getting cold and trying to warm itself by running around. Try for a controlled, rhythmical trot rather than an uncontrolled gallop.

This is an opportunity to say more about joint lubrication. Articular capsules become dry and inelastic from standing in the stall. Fluid is not produced to lubricate the joints until movement begins. Experts tell us that this procedure takes from ten to twenty minutes. This is why a horse coming from the stable should be ridden first at walk, and later in a relaxed trot. If you begin to trot or, worse yet, gallop too soon after mounting, you should not be surprised to find joint damage later. You should also know that some joint damage is undetectable, and lameness is not always obvious. By the time you can see signs of it, it is often too late to treat.

It follows then that young horses should not be allowed to run wild, because tendon and joint damage occur this way. When I speak of natural (or basic) trot I mean the way a horse trots when he is running loose without a rider. After you have lengthened the horse forward and downward at a walk and the horse has accepted the rein, you may begin trotting. When trotting, the horse should have light contact on both sides — known as long reins — but in no way should the mouth be worked, i.e., the horse should not be disturbed by the rider's hand.

In principle, always use a rising trot because it allows any tension to be directed forward and also helps to develop alertness in lazy horses. Remember, too, that for the horse to find balance you must always ride straight lines, never circles or voltes!

- *Remember:* Young horses must always be ridden in straight
  lines.

In the corners, which we round off, of course, at first, we let up on
the *outside* rein, leading inward with the *inside* rein, gently guiding the
horse around the corner. Ride the change of rein on the diagonal first
in a walk to avoid having to use force to pull the horse away from the
wall. In the walk phase, the reins should be loosened again and again
so that the horse can stretch and relax.

Two things are important during these first few days and weeks and
they are to ride straight lines and to ride forward. Indeed, the most
important rule of classical schooling is to point your horse straight
ahead and move forward. With all this attention given to forward
movement, the horse should not take off or get away from you. (Old
timers describe this as "running out from under the rider.") This can be
prevented by using a quiet voice, patting the horse, and by having light
contact with the reins.

At trot, too, the horse should always move with neck extended
forward and downward. Don't try to influence or straighten the neck as
this will cause the horse to tense his back and carry his head high,
thereby laying the basis for lower neck problems. Furthermore, because the horse's energy should never be overtaxed, don't trot too long
at first.

It is usually in these first days and weeks that irreparable mistakes
are made that later cause ambling paces, tense lower neck, stiff back,
neck throwing, head shaking, and tongue hanging, to name a few. Only
experienced riders will recognize these vices at the outset and know
how to avoid them.

The rider's hand should remain passive with light contact, relaxed
wrists, elastic fingers — no hard raw fist. One of the biggest mistakes in
this first phase of training is to want to get the horse on the aids and
gathered.

- *Remember:* The first "victory" over a young horse is won
  with a *passive* hand.

In principle it is best to work in a rising trot letting the knee and
thigh take over some of the work which will later be done by your seat
muscles and back. A beginner with an incorrect seat should never ride
a young horse — and yet it is often those riders who are not even

confident at the lowest level of dressage and who are not excellent riders yet who are drawn to a young, green horse.

If you are trotting with your horse and your horse offers a correct canter — i.e., a true-lead — let it happen. Sit a bit deeper in the saddle to show the horse the difference between this and the seat at trot. Do not *practice* cantering, but at the same time do not discourage it.

Goals of working in basic or natural trot:

1. The horse should be well-balanced.
2. The rider should drive the horse.
3. The horse should achieve rhythm.

Rhythm

A horse can only achieve rhythm when it is well-balanced with a rider astride and allows itself to be driven by the rider. The rider propels the horse using light, elastic leg aids. It is necessary to push down your heel because a lowered heel causes the calf to tense, and the calf must be tense to maintain contact with the horse.

Lazy horses should never be worked with a too active, or hammering leg. If necessary, it is better to use a whip as an aid. Nervous horses should be worked with *long* reprises at trot; lazy horses require many changes of tempo between walk, trot, and halt; temperamental horses should never be overstimulated. *Reprise*as used here in the equestrian sense means repetition of a lesson or pace.

When a horse finds a steady pace — i.e., its own tempo — then it has found its rhythm. This usually happens after about four to six weeks of work. Don't forget, however, that there are early and late bloomers. In the next few weeks your main task is to establish your horse's rhythm. A horse can only find its rhythm when leg and hand are used with sensitivity, with the rider helping the horse find and keep its rhythm. There are, of course, some horses who bring rhythm with them as a gift from heaven. In Germany, we say that these horses are born well-balanced.

When we speak of "rhythm" we are not referring only to uniformity of stride, but also to the precise simultaneous landing of diagonal pairs of legs at trot. If the forelegs hit the ground even a fraction of a second too soon, the horse is front heavy, and is therefore unbalanced and not in rhythm.

We will leave the familiarization phase now and move on to real training.

Standing still with reins resting on the horse's neck

Many inexperienced riders understand schooling to mean walk, trot, canter, and the dressage lessons. They forget that horses also have to learn to stand still. The horse already should have learned to stand calmly on the longe. It is also very important that the horse stand still when mounted. A horse that has not yet found its balance with the weight of a rider will have difficulty standing still at first, particularly for extended periods of time. For this reason it is very useful at the very beginning of a ride at walk to bring the horse repeatedly to a halt using voice and careful rein contact. At the same time give the horse the opportunity to find its balance while standing still. Do this by resting the reins carefully on the horse's neck. Praise your horse and do not shift weight as you allow the horse to stand quietly. To walk on, press slightly with both legs and help with a voice command ("walk on").

Although this lesson may seem silly to some riders, it is fundamental to training. Resist the urge to correct foot position if the horse stops in a slightly incorrect position. Later, when the horse has found its balance, it will *naturally* position itself correctly. The main purpose at this point of practicing standing still is for the horse to stand with completely loose reins, i.e., no support on the bit.

Now you can cultivate establishing balance during daily training by walking on a loose rein, trotting with slight contact, halting, and standing. Unfortunately, many horses, even older ones, have never learned to stand still while being mounted; you see it all the time. Some riders even consider a horse that runs away when being backed rather chic and sporty.

• *Remember*: Standing still is an important basic lesson.

Balance — underlying theme of basic schooling

One theme is constant throughout the previous chapters and that is balance. Although I have tried to avoid dry theory in this book, there are some concepts that are unavoidable for a rider/trainer.

You cannot train a young horse without *previously* informing yourself sufficiently about conformation, anatomical and physical movement processes, and the psyche of horses. For this reason this section should not be skimmed or skipped. The following comments lay the foundation for understanding subsequent training.

The subject of balance cannot be considered by itself, because other factors always play a role when we are talking about balance, for example, the power (drive) of the hindquarters, the horse's back, psychological constitution, and physical build (a rectangular or square horse). These are discussed in the next section dealing with suppleness and the horse's back.

When considering balance we differentiate between horizontal (side to side) and vertical (front to back) balance. In order to decrease swaying from side to side, we must deal first with horizontal balance. This can be achieved very quickly by riding on straight lines, first with the help of the wall. If the horse begins to sway, you must press forward; the more energetically you press forward, the closer the hind legs fall to the centerline — we say a correctly balanced horse is "narrow-tracked." The secret to finding balance, therefore, is to move forward and sit completely still in the saddle. Riding on the circle too early in training impedes finding balance.

Finding vertical balance (front to back) is usually more difficult and takes longer. It also requires a rider with more feeling and knowledge than is necessary to balance horizontally. This sensitivity cannot be learned in a few weeks or even a few years. This also explains why there are more poorly schooled horses than well-trained horses. Mastery of the "remount seat" (beginner's seat) is not enough, because sometimes the horse sways forward, sometimes backward. Rushing, overbending, and hanging on the hand are all problems resulting from balance difficulty; obviously, a horse cannot find its rhythm until these problems are overcome. Sensitivity and experience are necessary to correct these problems.

The horse uses its neck as a balancing pole. Thus, it should be allowed complete freedom to extend the neck when walking and should be ridden with very little contact at trot. The reins are only to make it easier for the horse to find its balance. The reins should never serve as a front support (like a fifth leg), nor at this stage of training should it be used to straighten your horse.

As long as we ride, we should never forget that the horse's motor is in the back — horses have rear wheel drive. All power comes from the hindquarters; the forequarters serve only as supports. This fact is important regarding every aspect of vertical balance; the hind legs *push* the horse forward. The farther back the center of gravity is, the more the hind legs are involved in *carrying*. This process is known as *collecting*.

One goal of training is to strengthen the hindquarters in such a way that the horse can bring back his center of balance to relieve the forequarters. A horse in his natural state carries fifty-five percent of his weight with the forelegs and forty-five percent with the hind legs. It is the task of a good rider to balance out this unfavorable ratio. With horses that forge, you can actually hear the increased strain; the horse lifts the foreleg from the ground too late. As a result the tip of back hoof touches and hits the foreleg. The only solution to this is to make the hind legs carry more weight. However, because the horse is not yet familiar with reins as aids at this early stage of training, this correction must be made by a skilled rider. When discussing pushing and carrying the hindquarters, it should be mentioned that in developing balance, the horse's back takes on the important function of a lever, directing the power forward from the hind legs. Even the best hindquarters are useless if there is anything wrong with the back, because this will cause difficulty with balance and suppleness.

In closing this section on balance, there are still several fundamental points to be made. There are as many balance problems as there are horses. Occasionally one encounters an enchanting creature that was born well-balanced, but you will also encounter many horses with a jarring action that will never be well-balanced. An experienced rider will be able to spot such an animal before purchase and will choose accordingly.

Psychological predisposition also plays a role in balance, as do the daily mood swings. Horses, too, are influenced by the weather and experience biological highs and lows. The old, often cited notion of the "stamina of a horse" is not valid; horses are often more delicate than humans, particularly when it comes to the digestive system.

* *Remember*: The first prerequisite for further work is a well-balanced horse.

Suppleness and the horse's back

In addition to balance, there is a second prerequisite for further schooling: suppleness. At first, it is natural for a young horse to tense and stiffen carrying the unfamiliar weight of a rider. By riding straight lines with a light seat, the horse should be able to establish balance with a rider while learning to trust its rider and dispel fear. Riding forward in a measured manner should give tight muscle groups a chance to relax, alternating relaxing and contracting. Only muscles that are not cramped can be adequately supplied with blood and fully ready for action. Relaxation work also helps make joints more pliant and breathing freer. Loosening a horse which has probably been standing in a stall or stable for twenty-four hours can be compared with the loosening up (or warm up) phase of track and field athletes, or the daily run for training in other sports.

Because the horse's back is the supporting bridge between the forelegs and the hind legs, it is here that a young horse is most likely to become tense. With this in mind, trainers of young horses must become familiar with the complexities of the horse's back. The elongation of back and neck forward and downward (stressed as the most important factor at walk with loose reins and at trot on straight lines with light contact) applies just as much to early *loosening work.* This elongation is the most important exercise for developing back muscles, and later for overall dressage training. For all subsequent work, note that horses that carry their heads too high or too low often develop back problems. If you concentrate on work that strengthens the back, the neck position will often correct itself. Horses with weak backs should be worked properly on a long longe before being mounted.

When discussing horses' backs we divide them into "back-goers" and "leg-goers." A back-goer relaxes its back more fully allowing for a supple back. A leg-goer refers to a horse with a stiff back which never, or only with difficulty, relaxes its back. Such horses are unsuitable for dressage.

Another conformation distinction is also often made between a "square horse" (short-backed) and a "rectangular horse" (long-backed), (see Figure 3). A rectangular horse is more suitable for dressage than a square horse because the relatively longer back of the rectangular horse is more likely to become supple.

A horse is supple when it moves in all three paces on a completely loose rein with full neck extension, a low frame, swinging tail, and supple back, without running away, i.e., it freely uses it's own body without resistance. A contented expression, snorting, and puffing are other indications of this relaxed state.

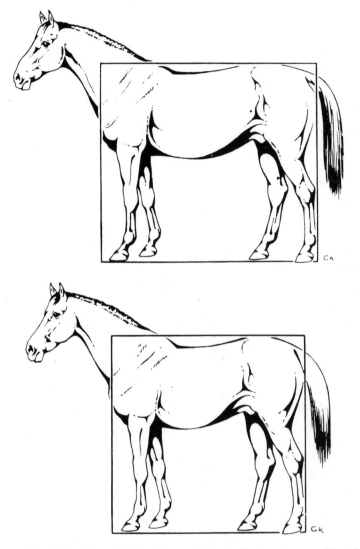

Figure 3. Top: Rectangular horse. Below: Square horse. (Reprinted from Knopfhart, A. 1987.)

How do you achieve this?
1. With longe work;
2. With free forward riding using passive rein and sensitive seat;
3. With cavaletti work — some horses also respond to open jumping;

4. The following suggestion is often useful for horses with extreme back problems and saddlephobia (or for older horses); let them run free without a saddle or rein, then saddle immediately afterwards and begin gentle work with a rider.

At first, the training consists entirely of loosening work (see section on loosening work). You cannot begin developmental work until the horse is well-balanced and supple.

* *Remember*:   You can barely hear a well-balanced, supple horse when it moves.

Introduction to lateral aids–riding on a circle

Because you cannot always ride in a straight line, young horses must also learn to go in a circle. As soon as the horse is fairly well-balanced on straight lines, begin working in a walk on a large circle. To do this bring the inside hand sideward toward the inside, and position your horse's head and neck slightly inside the leading rein. But first the outside hand gives slightly; the outer rein in this initial bending work should at first yield easily. Lean slightly inward with some weight on the inside stirrup (the first lateral weight aids). The inside leg is positioned about a hand's width behind the girth and works gently to push the haunches out. The outer leg does nothing, hanging passively at the horse's side.

This way the horse learns only the inside aids (inside rein and inside leg) so it moves without bending at the poll and has to find its center of gravity on the circle. At first, obviously, you cannot expect to keep exactly on the line of the circle, and you will probably ride this large circle in a zigzag.

Begin going to the left and do not demand too much. When you are satisfied that the horse has grasped the lesson, praise it, ride a straight line, and let it stretch. The next day practice going on the right hand. Later you can change more often, first walking, then trotting. At trot try to sit down for a few paces occasionally.

Other exercises for learning lateral sideward-driving aids are:

* turning on the forehand,
* large traversing voltes at walk,
* giving way to the leg with head to the wall.

All of these lessons are loosening exercises. Always remember that contact on the outside rein should be relatively light.

The goal of the lesson is to teach the horse that a leg *on* the girth effects *forward movement,* a leg *behind* the girth dictates *sideward movement.* Your horse should find a new center of gravity on the circle and carry more weight on the inside hind foot, thereby improving stride and posture. At the same time the horse learns lateral effects of the seat by the rider's stepping down in the stirrups. In this phase it is very important not to demand too much from your horse and to be satisfied with small successes.

- *Remember:*   The best reward for obedience is to dismount and lead your horse back to the stable.

From a natural trot to working trot

When your horse is loosened up through appropriate work, then it is time to do sitting trot for a few paces on occasion. You must always be prepared to return to a rising trot if the horse starts to tense his back again. (For approximately fifty years a rising trot has been called "English trot" in Germany and a sitting trot is known as "German trot.")

What is the difference between a natural (or basic) trot and working trot? In a natural trot we basically ride with a passive leg to the rhythm of the trot to allow the horse to achieve balance and rhythm. The working trot requires more work on the part of the horse than the horse would naturally offer without encouragement. So, the passive leg becomes active, the passive beginner's seat becomes a normal dressage seat, which in turn becomes a driving seat by bracing your back. The *active* leg is achieved by deeply flexing your heel down from your relaxed ankle. This automatically tenses the muscle in the calf that rests against the horse. Under no circumstances should you work your horse with your thighs or pulled up heels. A rider must have a deep, active seat to train a horse. In working trot, the rider determines tempo and rhythm — a measured and precise two-beat — one, two, one, two . . . The horse must be as regular as a clock ticks.

The hand is quiet and relaxed, as though you were balancing a glass of water and were afraid of spilling it. When in doubt, always let up rather than pulling in. If the horse is running off or speeding up, turn your wrist gently and brace your back, but don't use a hard hand.

Again a reminder here that we always begin each lesson at a walk with loose reins, then move to a relaxed rising trot, and then finally sit the working trot. If your horse is lazy, work many transitions from walk to trot. It is extremely important when working at trot to alternate with walking on loose reins so that the horse can stretch and relax. If your horse rears or runs away, concentrate on longe work. Never let a session become a power play.

Outside riding

Outside riding should be introduced at this stage of training. It should begin in the outdoor ring, and proceed at the same leisurely pace that it did in the indoor arena. Longeing, already begun, should also be shifted outdoors now. If a canter track is available, work your way around the track at a walk with a dependable lead horse, eventually adding occasional periods of trotting. If everything goes well, then try a few canter strides. All of this does not have to happen the same day; patience and self-control are absolute necessities. These first outdoor experiences should be entrusted to an unexcitable and dependable rider, rather than to someone who will not take the task seriously.

In today's training, outdoor riding is often neglected, and then the rider is surprised when, at his first competitions, his horse spooks or even goes out of control. Is this really surprising? Up until this point the horse has seen nothing but its stall and the indoor ring.

I know quite a few riders who have never been outdoors with their horses, not in five years, not in ten years. Their fear keeps them from doing so, and their mounts sense their insecurity. Their horses are poor creatures who know nothing but their stalls and the sandy indoor ring; when they are finally allowed out in the meadow, they go so wild that they come back in with swollen tendons and broken bones and are forced to stand around again.

We must not forget that a horse — like a human being — needs light, air, and outdoor exercise; it needs activity and a schedule. An ideal day for a horse is an hour of work on the track in the morning, better yet in the outdoor ring, followed by grooming and hoof cleaning out of doors, and then an hour outdoors in the afternoon or evening. The horses of bygone days, both cavalry and work horses, were healthier and more even-tempered not only because they worked more, but also because they had a regular daily schedule and were busy.

While we are on the subject of outdoors, we should emphasize a rule that seems to be unknown in most stables. Horses should always stand with their heads turned away from the stall door. Thus, mounting and dismounting outside the stall should never be undertaken with the animal's head facing the stall or stable, because horses when startled always run into or toward their stalls and the mounted rider can suffer serious injury. Also follow the old rule: Leave the stall in a walk; return to the stall in a walk.

Most riders know that horses should not trot or canter on hard surfaces like asphalt or cement, and they act accordingly. But these same riders trot or canter through spongy terrain without a thought, and many even use such terrain to make high-spirited mounts tired and docile. However, spongy terrain is even worse for horses' legs than hard surfaces, especially for young horses. Even newly constructed indoor rings or outdoor rings sometimes have fearfully dangerous spongy surfaces, so beware.

In concluding this section, it is necessary to make a few more remarks on outdoor riding. It is no secret that riders are not particularly popular in many circles. Time and again forest management professionals, hunters, farmers, fishermen, residents on the outskirts of towns, and hikers are alarmed and irritated by undisciplined riders. Every year you see hoof prints in freshly seeded areas or even in grain fields ready for harvest. People who cannot control their mounts have no place riding outdoors. On one novice trail ride I actually witnessed four out of eight riders falling off their horses at the edge of a ripe grain field and then saw their horses feeding in the field itself. The riders, also running through the field, then attempted to catch their mounts who naturally ran deeper into the field. It is easy to imagine what the field looked like at the conclusion of this. The increasing animosity toward riders that develops from events of this kind is easy to understand. Another deplorable custom on the part of riders is that instead of riding through puddles, which are very good for horses' hoofs, they ride around the edges of the puddles in ever-increasing rings that extend farther and farther into the field.

As already mentioned, the young horse should first go outdoors in the company of a placid and dependable horse. Excitement should be avoided as far as possible. Young horses often are afraid of large rocks, benches, puddles, baby carriages, agricultural machinery, and the like. There is only one cure for this. Guide the youngster quietly up to the object (possibly even dismounted), let him look at it closely and sniff at it, and remain calm. Punishment will achieve the opposite result and the horse's recalling of the frightening object will only be intensified by his memory of the punishment. On cross-country rides leave the dogs at home. They don't belong with you on outdoor rides, not on a leash, and above all not running free.

The most important rules for riding outdoors are summarized:

- Riding on footpaths and hiking trails is absolutely forbidden.
- If a pathway is used both as a hiking trail and a bridle path, then proceed at a walk on the extreme edge of the path.
- Where bridle paths are present, they must be used.
- Riding on harvested fields is permitted only with the permission of the owner, although permission is frequently tacitly given.
- When you meet hikers, bicyclers, and other riders proceed at a walk. Be courteous!

On the bit

Up until now we have ridden our youngster at a walk with a loose rein and at a trot with a very light rein (light contact); he has loosened up and already experienced weight and back pressure and an active leg. This light contact during the trot must now become more distinct and definite by stronger engagement of the horse's hind legs. Only a horse on the bit can be trained further; only a horse on the bit is obedient. Many riders are of the opinion that a horse does not need to be on the bit for a leisurely ride. This is a serious mistake, because a horse absolutely must be on the bit in street traffic or cross-country — especially on rough terrain, root-covered forest floors, areas with blind spots ahead — not only for the rider's safety, but also for the sake of others.

How do we put a horse on the bit? A horse is put on the bit by riding against the opposing rein with back and leg aids. That would appear to be a clear, comprehensible sentence; however, many riders do not know what the "opposing" rein is or how to achieve it.

From light contact we must carefully shorten the rein little by little, starting with the outer hand as when adjusting the reins. What we take up in front, we must balance with increased back pressure. The legs make sure that the gait remains energetic. Once we have found the right amount of rein, we then position the hands still and steady with the upper arms held vertically. For the time being we do not release the reins; but neither do we pull back. Most riders do not understand this instruction, and it is the first major error in putting a horse on the bit. The hand unconsciously draws back and the rider hangs on the reins.

We use both reins as if they were side reins; a side rein cannot give any slack (it is softly elastic because of the rubber rings), nor can a side rein pull the horse's head backward; it can only keep the position. Those who comprehend this can put a horse to the aids; those who hang on the reins will never learn this.

In putting the horse on the bit we place a relaxed, supple horse under a new pressure, but not undue stress; we apply pressure to the horse like a coil spring. The front end of the spring is the horse's mouth and the back end is his hocks, and it is on this extended, vibrating coil spring that we are sitting. By holding firm with the reins we prevent the front of the spring from shooting out, and with back and leg aids we prevent the spring from losing its tension in the back end.

Sooner or later the horse will give in to this tension in his neck, stop straining against the rein and withdrawing his back. At this point the horse has "flexed into the bit," i.e., flexed his jaw to accept contact with the bit. We say he has "reached for the ground" or taken a position "in hand." At this moment it is very important to praise the horse with your inside hand for submitting, while maintaining gentle but clear contact with the outside hand.

Now we can guide this horse on the bit more consciously with the hand and ride in the corners more distinctly than previously. To do this we need weight, the inside leg, and the outside rein. Riding through the corner we bend the horse around the inside leg with the inside hand and after the corner we straighten out again with the outside hand. In straightening out, we distinctly give with the inside hand in order to get the horse back on the outside, guiding rein. As soon as the horse wants to free itself from the bit, position both hands firmly again and apply back and leg aids.

Being placed on the bit is a lesson that every young horse must learn, but you should allow the horse enough time to comprehend this important lesson. A horse's mouth should never be worked with the hand, the horse should "reach for the ground," i.e., step into the bit on his own by giving with his neck. Patience is the basic principle for this training.

The training just described takes place at a trot. Do not put a horse at this stage of training to the aids at a walk. For the time being walk the horse only on a loose or long rein.

When your horse has accepted the bit, the highest point of the neck lies immediately behind the ears and the noseline is slightly in front of the vertical. The salivary gland by the horse's ear is stimulated in this position. The horse will begin to chew and foam will appear in the corners of its mouth.

Initially the lesson on the bit should not be too long because the horse will get sore muscles, resist, and be overstressed. That would be the basis for the following vices: "behind the bit," "against the bit," "wrong bend in the neck"—i.e., the poll is not the highest point of the neck— refusal, and tense lower neck.

Thus, we always allow the horse to stretch on the bit, to extend itself periodically and "reach for the ground"; and we must not neglect the requisite walking on a loose rein. Here the horse must learn to distinguish clearly that on the bit means work, and a loose or long rein means a break and relaxation. A horse trained like this will later have no difficulties in being put to the aids.

In addition, we must pay attention to a precise arm–hand position and the manner of holding the reins. The forearm, the backs of the hands, and the reins must form an unbroken line. In the transition from a trot to a walk we do not release the reins abruptly, but rather let the horse proceed a few strides in its old position and then open the hands, thus teaching the horse to chew the bit and only then give a completely loose rein.

This important stage of training does not always proceed as smoothly and problem free as we would like. The secret is to work on circles. Begin counterclockwise on a large circle, shorten the inside rein, and try to bend the horse toward the inside of the circle with its *lower jaw*. In doing so we must at first release slightly with the outside hand so that the horse can follow the bend to the inside.

Two things are important here: (1) the rider's inside leg must be placed firmly on the girth, and, (2) under no circumstances should the horse be led around by the neck. This means no bending of the neck, but rather a flexing of the lower jaw by means of taking up and releasing alternately with the inside hand while at the same time exerting strong pressure with the inside leg.

- *Remember:*   Bending (flexion) results from flexing of the
  lower jaw. If the horse is flexible in its lower jaw, then it
  will step into the bit on its own.

As soon as the horse gives with its lower jaw, the inside hand must yield and the outside rein must take the lead. In difficult cases the exercise just described must be done in a tighter circle at a walk. In doing this we must neither tighten the inside rein nor hold the outside rein too short.

Once you are successful in the circle then go large — i.e., ride the whole arena — using a sensitive inside hand. In putting the horse on the bit the center of gravity is shifted to the rear through the shortening of the neck and the tightened seat of the rider, so that the horse must re-balance itself in this new position. The reining technique here could be compared to a sliding weight scale used to measure chemicals. The upper sliding weight with the rough settings of 50 grams, 100 grams, 150 grams, etc., corresponds to the outside rein. Once we have determined the rough setting, then it snaps into place; in our case, the outside hand is positioned. The lower and smaller sliding weight with fine settings of 5, 10, 15 grams corresponds to the inside rein; it is not locked inflexibly into place, but it continues to balance the horse sensitively (with a gentle action of the fingers similar to squeezing a sponge), that is, through the light nibbling on the bit.

Here an explanation is in order. The novice rider is always told "Keep your hands still," "Don't move your hands," "Don't do anything with your hands," and these instructions are absolutely correct; however, there comes a time in a rider's career when the rigidly positioned fist must come alive and be a relaxed, sensitive hand. This is especially true for the *inside* hand. Those of you who want to train young horses must not only know these things, but you must be able to put these principles into practice.

- *Remember:*   Your hand must live with the horse's mouth.

This, however, is not the same as working the horse's mouth with the hand. Frequently, the difficulties that arise in connection with putting the horse on the bit disappear immediately or very soon after when the reins are held in one hand, because then the hands can no longer work the horse's mouth.

When your horse is making satisfactory progress and everything is in order, there is often a risk that the rider will not be able to call it a day because he wants to prolong the pleasure. The class should always end with a successful lesson so that the horse returns to his stall with a positive impression.

- *Remember*:   Only a few ever master the art of ending a
  lesson at exactly the right moment.

Avoid all training shortcuts. Basic training cannot be capriciously abridged. Even when so-called experts taunt you with things like "Are you ever going to get started with your horse?" or "Pack him in cotton and put him in a display case," continue steadfastly with tried and true classic basic training. By the time horses that have had time-tested basic training reach their best years, others who were started too early have long since made their way to the slaughterhouse. Unfortunately, today, there are more horses that end up at the slaughterhouse prematurely than there are horses who reach their best years.

In concluding this section, three questions must be answered: When is the horse on the bit? When is it on the aids? And is there a difference? Indeed there is a difference. On the bit has just been discussed in this section, i.e., in connection with bending at the lower jaw, contact, position in hand, and noseline. A horse that has been put to the aids is not only on the bit, but he is also under back and leg aids. A horse on the aids will always allow extension and collection, is obedient to forward-driving leg aids as well as lateral leg pressure. It reacts to every change in the rider's seat, collecting itself, and responding to any half-halts. But *your* youngster is not yet in this stage of training; to reach this stage it needs still more basic training.

Loosening (or suppling) lessons

In previous chapters, I have used the term "supple" repeatedly to describe how young horses — and all horses for that matter — should move. This stage is reached by allowing the horse to stretch downward and forward in an elongated position and by returning to walking with loose reins again and again.

In training young horses, we distinguish between suppling exercises and collecting exercises. The main difference is that suppling exercises are primarily ridden using the inside aids. For instance, on the large circle you bend the horse using the *inside* rein around the *inside* leg, at first even with the inside hand moved to the side. The outside hand does nothing, actually letting out; the outside leg also remains passive.

Collecting exercises employ the outside, outer rein and outer leg aids *in addition.* This places the horse under more pressure. In collected bending exercises, for example, increased pressure of the bit on the lower jaw is the result of equal application of the outside rein. Furthermore, bringing the outside leg back causes the rear half of the backbone to bend. Consequently, we differentiate between *suppling* exercises (first-degree bending) in which the horse is only flexed at the lower jaw (flexion) and *collected* bending exercises (second-degree bending) in which the entire spine is supposed to be curved around the inside leg. A dressage level volte with longitudinal bend is thus a collecting exercise, while the traversing volte — unfortunately very much a figure of the past — in which the horse traverses with the hind legs to the outside (in a shoulder-in position) — is a suppling exercise.

All work at walk where traversing is allowed can be used to supple a horse. Increasing and decreasing squares in which the horse is supposed to move with the entire spine in a longitudinal bend is the beginning of collected work.

In the section "Introduction to Lateral Aids," the loosening exercises such as turning on the forehand, traversing volte, and leg yielding are described. But here I will be more specific about leg yielding.

To prepare for leg yielding, start off at walk around the whole arena with slight flexion to the outside on the long side. Pull the inside leg back and press the hind legs away from the wall as soon as your horse lets up in the lower jaw. The leg should be activated only at the exact moment the horse pushes off with the inside hind leg, because it is only in that precise moment that the aid will be effective. If your horse tries to get away, then check him with the outside rein, using the inside rein to maintain the flexion to the inside.

- *Remember*: The leg aid works to drive the hind leg on the same side forward and/or sideward *only at the moment of push off.*

A serious, widespread error when practicing leg yielding is to pull the horse around by the neck. The horse should be straightened and move with only slight flexion in the lower jaw. The outside leg rests passively behind the girth prepared to check sideward movement if necessary. In the beginning you must be satisfied with the slightest progress. Any use of force risks damage to tendons and joints. The greatest angle of the horse's body with the wall should be forty-five degrees, although twenty-five to thirty degrees is preferable. Both horse and rider can learn a lot from leg yielding but a great deal of damage can be done too. I say again, only really experienced riders should train young horses.

- *Remember*: "Walks" in the pasture, letting your horse run free, and incorrect leg yielding are how vets make their money.

(*Comment:* There is no question that young horses need to be walked in the pasture because it helps them in the sudden transition from pasture to stall. But it is also true that many horses suffer injuries in the pasture. The reasons are (a) inappropriate fencing (barbed wire), (b) they are left in the pasture with horses they don't get along with, or (c) neighbors throw spoiled or inappropriate food in the pasture, for example moldy bread, bad carrots, grass from the lawn mower. In Part III, in the section, "What is lameness and what causes it?" I will discuss letting horses run free.)

Leg yielding has the following goals:

- introduction to the sideward driving leg,
- introduction to the outside opposing leg,
- finding balance in forward, lateral movements.

In addition, leg yielding is an excellent help in putting the horse on the bit. But you should avoid practicing leg yielding too often or for too long at a time. A few paces just to check the sideward-driving leg should be enough at a time.

There are many ways to loosen a horse and here, too, the trainer's years of experience are of utmost importance. Try to avoid strict inflexible training programs. Many horses loosen up in long periods at walk with slightly extended posture. Skilled riders also use a sitting, collected trot to warm up. This method is often necessary with horses who forge or have a tendency to make a noise caused by air in the sheath. When a horse that forges is tired or moving with too much weight forward, the tips of the hind feet hit the hoofs of the forelegs. The only solution is to sit down and shift more weight to the hind legs.

I know of a "crazy" horse who always went wild during lessons, bucked back and forth across the arena, and never became supple. He was a hopeless case that stymied the rider. The following procedure helped. The horse was led to the arena and mounted. Then the rider and horse stood completely still for ten to fifteen minutes, while the other horses were working. Then the horse was ridden around the arena at a walk on a long rein. This treatment produced a supple horse. Of course we all know many so-called experienced riders who would advise in such a difficult case, "All he needs is a good beating once in a while!" A beating is hardly a solution for a horse that won't relax.

The following exercises are for loosening or suppling:

- Walk on a loose rein or with light contact;
- Rising trot with light contact;
- Large circle with serpentines and lower jaw bending, but no longitudinal bending;
- Turning on the forehand;
- Leg yielding (straightened horse with slight lower jaw bending);
- Traversing voltes;
- Cavaletti work;
- Canter work in ordinary canter, maybe with a light seat.

Often, lengthening and shortening (change of tempo in trot) and jumping over low obstacles are also considered loosening exercises. I do not agree with this, particularly with young horses, because too frequently I have experienced young horses, already loosened up, who get excited and tense up in changes of tempo at trot and during jumping.

Be careful not to think of any of these lessons and figures as an end in themselves, but rather use them as tools to supple and exercise your horse. You will also use them in later training, returning to them whenever your horse is tense. In fact, most of each lesson with a young horse should be devoted to loosening or suppling work, gradually shortening the amount of time spent on it.

- *Remember*:   The road to success requires an attentive, but relaxed, contented horse.

A few words must be said here about use of the whip and spurs in lessons involving turning on the forehand, leg yielding, and traversing voltes. You should not use spurs for the next few months of training. They should not be introduced until you reach collected training. However, you should familiarize your horse with the whip early on in training. If you have used a short whip on the horse's shoulder during the first week, then you will need a dressage whip for the sideward-driving lessons. In principle, it is used to *supplement* the leg aid, should always be directly behind the leg, and should be used simultaneously. In most cases, a light touch is sufficient. If a young horse resists the leg and does not respond to the whip either, it is a sign that it may be too early for that lesson. Continue to work on basic training—without punishment or beatings, but firmly and patiently.

Drive and initial elevation of the forehand (lengthening and shortening in trot)

Before beginning this section, a few terms must be defined: gait, drive, and impulsion. *Gait* refers to the natural tendency of the horse to move forward in the three paces, with or without rider. Gait is a judgement of the quality of the horse. We distinguish between regular or irregular, enthusiastic or dragging, free or tight gait. *Drive* is essentially the powerful *push off* from the ground by the hind legs. It is not so much natural as a result of the training effect by the rider. *Impulsion* develops from the drive of the hind legs (elasticity of paces when pushing off and landing) and from a supple back. Impulsion is impossible if movements are tense.

We use extending exercises followed by shortening exercises to develop powerful hindquarters. The term *hindquarters* takes on special meaning for the rest of basic training. Never forget that the horse's motor is in the back. (The German word for hindquarters is "hinterhand" and originally comes from equestrian jargon meaning that which is behind the hand of the rider. In dressage, the word "hindquarters" refers to the entire rear locomotor system to the hip.) Before beginning changes of tempo in trot, the rhythm in working trot must be absolutely secure. At this point the first goal is to *lengthen* the working trot in short sessions, not to learn a medium trot.

Of course, this transition into lengthening of stride in the same rhythm is preparation for the medium trot later, but for now concentrate on practicing nothing but acceleration.

To develop drive, carefully tighten both calves and push the horse on while giving a somewhat lower outside hand. In most cases, it will be enough to let the horse clearly feel the calf and perhaps the tip of the whip. Your horse will comprehend most easily immediately after straightening out from the second corner of the short wall. Gradually, in a supple horse, drive becomes impulsion, a powerful but elastic hind leg push-off from the ground.

Shorten again after a few steps by bracing the back against a very passive hand. At the same time push more weight to the hind legs, because they must carry more. This lesson should teach the horse that lengthening means *push* and shortening means *carry*.

This initial "carrying" is the horse's first lesson in collection. In addition, increased load lowers the hindquarters somewhat, the horse has a feeling of being larger in the front, and raises its forehand. This initial elevation of the forehand, also known as relative or natural elevation, takes place against a *passive* hand. The rider should feel like he is riding uphill.

- *Remember*: Elevation is a result of increased weight on the hind legs.

A major error in training at this phase is to try to achieve this elevation using active hand movements. Later elevation against a higher positioned hand, referred to as active or absolute elevation, is not possible until the hindquarters are sufficiently strong.

Again and again we see riders practicing lengthening and shortening who do not have the leg on the horse when shortening. The result is that the hind legs do not step under the center of gravity to carry the weight. Impulsion gives way to flat, pitiful paces. The whole purpose of the exercise is missed, and worse still, the rider doesn't even know it because he cannot feel it. When this happens, it is the beginning of the end of the young horse's training, for the future will hold nothing but flat, sloppy gaits.

- *Remember*: Without impulsion there is no elevation.

Flexion, bending, angle (introduction to the outside aids)

A book about how to train young or green horses has to be divided into separate sections in order to give the reader an overview. But, by organizing the material in this way, I run the risk that an inexperienced rider might think the training has to follow this strict plan. In reality, many separate phases of training and lessons overlap. So, for example, in the lessons on turning on the forehand and leg yielding we have already dealt with the *outside* leg, and you have already heard about *bending* on the circle in the section about putting the horse on the bit.

Several terms must be defined before continuing in this section: flexion, bending, and angle. *Flexion* refers to the bend of the head through the neck when the horse is straight. It involves nothing more than bending the lower jaw with no opposition from the outside rein to speak of, whereby the neck should be as straight as possible. The outside rein simply *prevents* the neck from over bending. By *bend* we mean longitudinal bending of the entire spine from the neck to the root of the tail using the *outside* rein and leg aids. When riding circles, the long axis of the horse should be lined up exactly with the track to be ridden. The neck should never be curved more than the rest of the spine, and since the spine only bends slightly, the neck should not be flexed much either. The *angle* is the distance at which — in sideward steps — the forehand (or hindquarters) is positioned from the track of the hind legs (or forelegs). With young horses, the angle should equal no more than one step.

Now on with the training of your young horse. He is already familiar with first-degree bending (flexion) using mainly inside aids. In this first bending phase the neck should be firmly locked to the shoulder. A loose neck makes all further work difficult, if not impossible. A horse uses his neck as a balancing pole and the rider needs it later as a lever for elevation. (Sometimes a horse uses his tail to help balance, as well.) The muscle on the crest of the neck of a correctly flexed horse should move from one side to the other as the horse strides out. Often lower jaw and parotid gland problems make flexion difficult. When buying a horse always check to make sure that the horse is good through the jowl. Think twice about a horse with a short, fat neck.

Now we get to the longitudinal bending of the entire spine and with it the use of the outside aids. The effect of the outside rein comes through the inside rein. The outside leg is not effective until giving in to inside leg pressure. Turning on the forehand and leg yielding are good lessons for finding the outside leg (which regulates the placement of the hind leg) and the outside rein (which checks and regulates the neck's flexion).

- *Remember*:   A horse should not find the outside aids until
  he gives in to the inside aids.

It is best to begin longitudinal bending of the entire spine on a large circle. The inside leg is placed on the girth as the center of the longitudinal bend. The inside rein flexes the horse's lower jaw and bends the front half of the spine. The outside leg behind the girth bends the rear half of the spine around the inside leg. To start, be satisfied with a slight bending. Later, decrease the size of the circle and ask for increased bending. Then you will have reached the goal of second-degree bending. Do not work at this for long periods of time. Intersperse these exercises with straight lines to straighten the horse and freshen impulsion.

The inside leg, as the most important aid in bending, has three jobs: (1) forward driving, (2) keeping the horse from pushing toward the inside, and (3) acting as a supporting column around which to bend.

The outside leg *helps* forward drive. The outside rein first limits the neck bend and then takes over as the *leading* rein. The horse must learn to maintain this inside bend even when the inside rein lets up periodically. This *letting up* with the inside hand and *picking up* with the outside hand as leading rein is discussed in the section "On the Bit."

The basis for all bending work is riding on the circle in a brisk working trot with a correctly flexed horse. The horse must learn to stay exactly on the line of the circle. It may only *touch* the points of contact on the wall and may not shove into the corners. Circle points used to be called "halt points," because it was on these points that a horse would be stopped on the circle with an appropriate halt.

Once your horse is fairly secure on the circle, decrease the size of the circle. This is not accomplished by pulling in with the inside rein but by employing the *outside* leg and rein (introduction to firmer outside aids).

Practice large voltes in the corners and at the same time help your horse to accept the bit on the track going both to the right and to the left. Later we will expand this exercise to include half circles with change of rein.

A supple horse is a prerequisite for all bending work. A tense, tight back will not bend. Therefore, whenever your horse begins to tense up, you must get it to loosen up before continuing. As with everything else in basic training, we begin bending work on the horse's good side.

Regarding application of the outside aids it should be mentioned that they are used not only for bending, but also as opposing aids. For example, firm application of the outside rein on the horse's neck will prevent the outside shoulder from falling out. The outside leg behind the girth prevents the hindquarters from moving outside. Picture in your mind that the outside aids form a line along which the horse must move.

A horse that has been correctly worked in longitudinal bending will get visible vertical wrinkles on its neck. Work on the circle is also an introduction to another important section of training, hind leg gymnastics. Correct longitudinal bending on the circle requires increased engagement with the hind legs strengthening the respective hind leg. In addition to improving the bending of your horse's spine by working on a circle, you can also exercise the hind legs, a by-product, so to speak, of correct circle work.

By now you are aware of the fact that work on the circle represents a very important phase of training. Steinbrecht's book, *Gymnasium des Pferdes,* devotes 80 pages to bending work. All the more surprising that so many riders know so little about it. They start to get bored when the lesson moves to correct circle work or they get an arrogant, condescending expression on their faces that says they think this is a pedantic, old–fashioned method. Later it often becomes apparent that these are the very riders who cannot tell the difference between circle and transition points.

If this seems like exaggeration, take a look at a riding ring. You will notice by the ruts in the track that hardly anyone rides proper corners. Most begin the corner and the large circle at the same transition point. They go round and round just moving the horse. I recently witnessed a dressage test. Of nineteen participants, only fifteen could ride an exact circle and none could manage decent corners. These riders had apparently never heard of flexion or longitudinal bending either. To my amazement, almost all of the candidates passed the test. A rider who has not yet mastered basic training and who cannot even ride the whole school or a correct circle should not be awarded a medal.

For another example, a judge at a German tournament told me that in one test at the show only six of twenty-seven participants rode a perfect serpentine on the long wall (see Figure 4). At a press conference at the 1986 CHIO Donaueschingen, "Old master" Hans-Günter Winkler made the following grave statement, "We are practically devoid of complete training from bottom to top." These incidents show what has become of basic training. Where are young horses to get solid training when their riders haven't even mastered the basics?

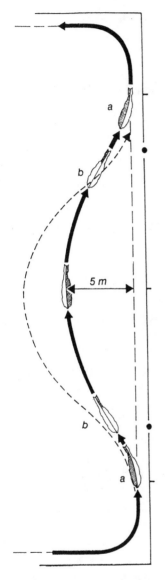

Figure 4. Simple serpentine:
one loop on the long side.
➡ Correct
– – – Incorrect
a/b Changing the bend.
(Reprinted with the kind
permission of the German
Riding Association, Warendorf,
from *Richlinien für Reiten
und Fahren,* Vol. I,
Grundausbildung für
Reiter und Pferd.)

Let us return to bending work with serpentines (see Figure 4). Turning on the circle is not accomplished by pulling the horse around with
the inside rein, but by applying weight. Most riders will know this as a
test question on riding tests but only a few understand the concept of
using weight as one of the aids. So it is not a matter of where you bend

your horse, but rather where you shift your center of gravity. The procedure is similar to riding with no hands on a bicycle.

- *Remember*:   A horse always steps under the rider's center of gravity.

The rider's seat must be correct and knee and thigh must be glued to the saddle for lateral weight to be an effective aid. To turn on a straight line (as on the serpentines) we must distinguish between three types of weight aids:

1. A light step in the stirrup;
2. A perceivable weight on the inner seat bone, in addition to the step in the stirrup;
3. Body turned toward the new direction, primarily with the thighs and knees.

The inside shoulder is pulled back somewhat in this bent seat. The inside rein helps the turn in that the horse must be curved. The outside rein on the horse's neck presses the horse into the curve but in such a manner that the outside hand never goes across the withers.

An excellent lesson for rider and horse is riding serpentines at a working trot in the whole arena or later as a two-loop serpentine along the long wall. Here are the aids: alternating leg, stepping into the stirrup, inside shoulder lowered and pulled back, and alternating longitudinal bending in harmonious agreement with the movement. These serpentines, as well as three-loop serpentines on the long wall resemble a dance with the horse: waltz to the left, waltz to the right . . . When ridden skillfully and elegantly, the horse will soon enjoy it too. Be careful with the outside hand. It must give sufficiently when bending; many riders hold too firmly on the outside, hindering flexion in the lower jaw. The result is that the horse gets behind the rein or gives up. The cardinal error in all bending work is too much hand and too little shifting of the weight. Many don't ride at all; they "drive." It is not so much whether you ride your horse on the circle but rather *how* you ride it. Mastering the bending seat described above will require years of work and effort.

Straightening also belongs in this discussion about bending. Almost all young horses are "crooked." At first you are powerless against the crookedness of a young horse. Not until your horse has learned to answer the outside aids and is familiar with bending exercises are you in a position to straighten out your horse.

A horse is not straight until the drive from the hind legs can go directly toward the center of gravity and straight across the straightened spine into the neck. On a curve, the horse is considered straight when the hind legs and forelegs step in the same track. This is called "straight on a curve" or "straight on a circle."

Horses are narrower in the shoulders than in the hips. If it is being ridden in a straight line along the wall and its shoulder and hip are the same distance from the wall, then the inside hind leg is not stepping under the weight, but next to it on the inside. When you apply the outside rein to the shoulder, the forelegs will shift more toward the inside, *in front of* the hind leg track. Unfortunately, many riders training young horses have never heard of this. Using this method — forelegs in the tracks of the hind legs — should put an end to all leg yielding and all sideward steps, even a horse cantering on two tracks should be corrected in this manner.

- *Remember*: When straightening out, the forelegs are always aligned with the track of the hind legs — not vice versa.

In closing this most important section on bending, I will summarize the main points.

Developing bending work

- Use lateral aids as loosening exercises;
- Use additional outside aids to introduce the horse to lateral bending;
- Increase the outside aids to improve bending, gait, carriage and to begin collection.

Important points about longitudinal bending

The arc must go through the entire spine *evenly*. Don't pull the neck around but lock the neck to the shoulder. When problems arise, ride forward with determination. It is possible that the outside rein may be too tight; if tension is present, loosen the horse first and increase work on the difficult side.

- *Remember:* The horse must be equally smooth on both sides and allow itself to bend.

Developing the canter

As mentioned in preceding sections, when a young horse offers a correct canter on its own you should not discourage it. But pay attention to inside bending and correct seat, so that the horse understands the canter from the beginning.

In order to learn to canter, the horse must already be familiar with the outside aids, that is, it must be able to bend. We distinguish between two possibilities for beginning the canter: (a) Offering a canter depart from a rising trot and, (b) offering a canter depart from a sitting trot.

Cantering from a rising trot

A young horse will best comprehend the transition from a rising trot to canter through extension. Ride a large circle at a rising trot, beginning preferably on the left diagonal. Then position the horse in a distinct flexion to the inside and, as you rise, quickly and energetically bring *only the inside hip* forward. At the instant of this action with the inside hip, concentrate somewhat more on flexion to the outside and drive more energetically with the inside leg while drawing the passive outside leg slightly back. Continue a rising trot, extending with the inside hip until the horse steps out. At this instant, the inside hand must let the stride out and the rider gets into canter seat. The primary impulse for this comes from the acceleration of the inside half of the body, which interrupts the double beat of the trot.

Initially, canter for only a short time, and alternate often between the trot and the canter. Do not return to canter until after the horse calms down at a trot. Under no circumstances should the horse find the canter an upsetting gait — a risk that exists especially with high-spirited horses. At the beginning of this work, practice on only *one* side. Do not start on the other side until a day or two after the canter has been stabilized on the first lead.

Naturally, this initial cantering can take place outdoors on a large circle, but it should be a suitable surface; it should not be soggy or too spongy. In order to go from a canter to a trot, settle into a trotting seat and curb the inside legs by means of short inside-rein movements. It must be emphasized that at this stage of training the horse must not canter in tight circles or turns, because the outside front leg, which bears all the weight at first, could be easily injured.

Cantering from a sitting trot

In preparing to canter first bring the horse into a shortened trot, also called a slow working trot. It is interesting to note that there are several intermediate teaching stages between a young horse's working trot and the later collected trot. Regrettably, trainers these days scarcely mention the slow trot, much less bother to teach it.

The *slow trot* is a slightly collected working trot in preparation for a collected trot. The hindquarters, which have pushed off up until now, are bent more and must carry more weight. The horse raises its head on its own (relative elevation) elevating the action of the forelegs.

The slow trot is developed from a brisk working trot and is achieved by using repeated half-halts from a deep seat and with braced back. Give the horse a somewhat exaggerated flexion to the inside, then straighten up using the outside rein and an opposing inside rein; at the same time the leg aids bring up the hind legs. The feeling of suppleness on the inside must not be lost; the gait must have impulsion and energy and should not drag. Once the slow trot has been achieved, the rider must sit still, being careful not to disturb the horse. At first we must be satisfied with only slight improvement at the slow trot, being careful to ride at this gait for only short stretches. It must always be followed by an energetic working trot. In principle, the slow trot is developed from a brisk working trot, preferably after preliminary extension.

The old "Riding Regulations of 1912" (HDv. No. 12) note the following regarding slow trot:

> In the slow trot the horse should take higher steps and cover less
> ground, but the paces should not be pounding or hovering. Since it
> flexes its haunches more, it carries itself higher, combining the
> greatest collection with the greatest throughness.[*]

[*] ["Throughness is beyond just a responsiveness to the rider's aids. Put simply, it comes when the horse is straight and allows the action of the reins to come "through" the whole body enabling it to move in the most expressive way its natural gaits will allow." Felicitas v. Neumann-Cosel, ed., *Ahlerich*, Middletown. MD: Half Halt Press, 1986. — Trans.]

Many horses seek to avoid this uncomfortable collection by leaning on the rein; others do so by creeping behind the rein and moving forward with short, flat steps. Consequently, do not ride the slow trot for too long. Short stretches of free paces should be interspersed. If the horse leans on the rein, then the rider must prompt it to carry itself better by means of short half-halts and correcting the neck and head set. A tapping rather than squeezing action of the legs, especially the inside, also helps. If the horse creeps behind the rein, then the rider must use leg aids to drive it forward and increase tempo in order to regain contact.

It is amazing how important the slow trot was thought to be in those days, and even more amazing that there is scarcely a rider today familiar with it.

The dressage canter

When cantering with a young horse we must distinguish between two phases, the preparation phase and the actual canter. To prepare for the canter, ride a circle at a slow trot, working on the easy side first. The inside hand keeps the inner side smooth while the outside hand tries to shift more weight to the outside hind leg. The inside leg is on the girth and the outside leg is behind the girth. When the horse is moving with longitudinal bending it is ready to canter. The actual canter is executed by pressing the inside hip and inside seat bone forward on one side thereby shifting more weight to the inside hind leg; at the same time, the inside leg drives more forcefully forward, trying to interrupt the regular trotting movement by tapping lightly. Make sure from the very beginning that the actual help in moving the horse out comes from the hip and seat.

If the horse lifts itself, then let the first stride out with the inside wrist while the outside hand maintains contact. Every subsequent stride must be forced forward using the inside hip, seat, and leg. Cantering is best done on the open side of the circle along the long wall. The stride should move freely forward. Do not canter too long and do not demand too much at a time. Occasionally, ride around the entire track at a brisk working trot.

When cantering, the spine of the horse should follow the curve of the circle; the outside hand remains still (as if balancing a full glass of water). The seat must also be immobile and supple. Never try to help by rocking the upper body back and forth.

- *Remember*:   Longitudinal bending and self-carriage are prerequisites for dressage canter.

Be especially careful to make the inside hip the primary aid when asking for a canter; your inside leg aid helps draw the inside hind leg forward, and a short rein movement on the outside checks the outside hind leg in its step forward. Thus, you achieve increased forward and downward movement of the inner hind leg.

In response to the question of how to use the aids for canter, one often hears. "You ask for a canter by moving the outside leg back." This answer is not totally correct, because moving the outside leg back is actually a bending exercise. If you teach your horse to canter when the outside leg is moved back, it will canter every time you want to trot on a circle or turn on a volte. This would make a decent longitudinal bending at a walk or a trot impossible.

- *Remember*:   While the outside leg flexes and announces the canter, the inside leg and hip provide the actual impulse (one-sided back bracing).

When first working at canter, practice on only one lead. Once the horse understands the aids, introduce the other lead. Later change leads often to consolidate what has been learned. Do not punish a horse that does not understand immediately, and be generous with praise when it is cooperative and willing to learn.

The canter is correct when the rider has a sensation of riding uphill. Moreover, when cantering on hard surfaces, you can hear if the horse is stepping correctly: The canter has a three-beat rhythm: one, two, three — one, two, three. Your horse is moving out correctly with his inside weight-bearing hind leg under the center of gravity when the stress of the three beats is on the *second* beat: one, *two*, three — one, *two*, three. If the stress is on the *third* beat: one, two, *three* — one, two, *three,* then the horse is putting too much weight on the forehand. Take the word "tremendous" as a memory aid; you notice that the stress in this word is on the middle syllable: tre-*men*-dous. When the stress is like this, the horse is cantering correctly. But note the stress pattern in the word "humoresque," with the stress on the last syllable: hu-mor-*esque.* If this is the rhythm you hear, the horse is on the forehand.

The transition from canter to trot is obtained through short rein movements on the inside with lightly braced back, making sure to keep the hind legs well forward. Later we will ride the entire arena at a canter. At that time use both legs to ask for long, steady strides. Note that the legs must work with the strides. The rider's gaze is *forward* and *upward*. The gaze upward is very important for developing a correct canter seat. Once the horse can stay on track, then you can take the rein in one hand from time to time.

When the canter is completely mastered, then you can begin it in the middle of the short side and later on the long side. You must have an impeccable seat and never lean forward. You are not yet ready to practice a canter on the middle line, that is, without lining up against the wall, because there is a risk that the horse will not be straight. Even cantering on the long wall we must be careful that the horse does not go at an angle or canter on two tracks. To verify this the trainer stands in a corner and watches the horse head-on as it comes down the wall of the arena. Straightening out was already mentioned in the section "Flexion, bend, angle." If your horse is cantering on two tracks, then place the forelegs somewhat inside in front of the hind legs — ideally we imply the "shoulder in" concept. Cantering on two tracks must be stopped immediately, because this easily becomes a bad habit with many horses.

Before cantering cross-country the rider must decide whether to canter on the left lead or on the right lead, and then position the horse accordingly. This decision should never be left to the horse.

Of course, once the horse is used to the easy side, he must also practice more on the difficult side; the basic rule in all dressage work is that both sides must be worked equally.

What if your horse strikes off into incorrect canter? Canter training does not always go according to the book. We must analyze where the problems lie. If the horse strikes off incorrectly again and again, then in most cases it is because something is wrong with bending on the circle at a trot. Remember that horses also have a good side and a not-so-good side. If the horse's and rider's bad sides are the same, problems are likely to occur. For instance, many riders sit off balance and don't even know it. Often a young horse makes his rider aware of a faulty seat. In such cases the first thing to do is to correct your seat.

If your horse strikes off into canter incorrectly, then calmly come back to a slow trot , maintain it for a few strides, and canter again with renewed, more distinct aids. If the horse continues to go into a canter incorrectly despite correct seat and aids, try the following corrections:

1. Go back to striking into canter by extending out of a rising trot.
2. Same as above, but ride at a rising trot on the *wrong* diagonal on the circle and lay a rail on the ground on the long side to interrupt the two-beat rhythm.
3. Ride the whole arena at a sitting trot — just before the first corner of the short side adopt *exaggerated* flexion to the inside and at the moment the horse strikes into canter turn the horse to the outside (rider twists slightly to the outside).
4. Go into a canter from a volte in trot.
5. Decrease the size of the circle slightly at a slow trot with firm flexion to the inside and, while increasing the circle after the closed side, strike into a canter.
6. Ride out of the corner at a slow trot, with active inside leg. At the instant of change (just before the wall) strike off into canter with energetic aids.

All corrections should seek to hold back the outside pair of legs. This takes place with hearty rein movements on the outside from the wrist (not from the arm). The active, *forward-driving* inner leg pressure calls the inside pair of legs forward, and the inside hand releases the stride. Many failures in cantering are because the inside hand is holding the horse too tightly. Try not to bog down on this lesson if you encounter problems. Just continue to work steadily on basic training and one day success will come suddenly as if by itself. This is also true for other lessons such as leg yielding, standing still on all four legs, rein back, and later for the medium trot, pirouettes, and counter canter.

If basic training is correct, then the results often fall into the rider's lap at a later date like fruit from a tree. However, basic training should not be shortened or changed arbitrarily. When problems arise, always keep in mind that there are precocious horses as well as late bloomers, and there are also many horses with serious physical defects.

The medium canter

To lengthen the canter strides, it is necessary for the inside leg particularly to work more energetically *with* the stride, and for the inside rein to release longer strides. The outside rein must maintain throughness using short movements. Increasing the tempo does not actually mean going faster, but rather that the strides grow longer, while at the same time remaining steady and even. In the medium canter the rider must remain deep in the saddle (inner seat bone) and go smoothly with the movement.

The simple change of leg in canter

In order to prepare for and to master the simple change of leg in canter, the horse must be familiar with (and obey) halts, thus demonstrating that it is responsive and "through." From this point of view, it is too early in training to introduce the simple change. However, to give continuity to the chapter, I will discuss this important lesson at this juncture. (Collected canter will be discussed in the chapter on collection).

The simple change of leg in canter—when correctly executed—is not an easy exercise, because it requires absolute throughness from the horse. This explains why it is not included in lowest level dressage tests or the 1986 edition of the exercise book. One of the biggest mistakes in this lesson is trot steps in between, before the horse moves into a walk or canter. Another major error is "taking a running start" when striking into canter. These two errors are by no means the only problems, but they are the most conspicuous and the most serious .

The first preparation for simple change of leg consists of practicing transitions, e.g., canter-walk-canter on the circle. Beginning with a free working canter, the strides are gathered slightly using the back weight and outside rein, thereby preparing the horse for the halt. Now comes a definite, but not too harsh, transition to a walk. The objective has been achieved when your horse goes to a walk immediately without trotting in between. In practicing this lesson make sure to ride at a walk for a long time, because thewalk should be regular and smooth before going into a canter again. When work has progressed to a point where you are satisfied with the walk after just a few steps (six to eight), you can pull up shortly before reaching the track, leave the circle in walk, and strike into canter. Perfect aids—noticeable pressure on the inside seat bone and a forward inside hip—are prerequisites for the success of this lesson. Eventually, shorten the walking phase gradually until you are down to two or three regular steps.

In practicing the simple change there is some risk that the horse will anticipate the rider's aids or tense up. If this happens, break off work immediately and work at a walk or a trot allowing your horse to forget about change of leg in canter for the time being. Also in preparatory work on the circle (changing between canter and walk), change leads often and practice the exercise on the whole arena so that the horse will not anticipate the aids. If you have difficulties, go back to a brisk working trot; don't become obsessed with a simple change of leg in canter. Another error that often creeps into the work is when the horse goes on two tracks at changes in flexion. When this happens we go back to working on the circle with very long stretches of walking.

It is best to incorporate the simple change of leg into the daily routine occasionally without practicing it too frequently. This is, incidentally, true for many lessons, particularly for turning out of a halt and reining back.

Halts

Before discussing the halting aids, I must explain what halts really are. Those of us who have been training horses and teaching riding for years and even decades know that there is either a tremendous gap in today's riding instruction, or there is a very imprecise definition of halts being offered. The confusion relates primarily to the half-halt. There is less confusion regarding the complete halt.

> Complete halts are the result of half-halts that bring the horse to a stop from all gaits. When coming from a higher gait the complete halt is supported by the immediately preceding half-halt. The complete halt is only executed on a straight line. (*Richtlinien für Reiten und Fahren*, FN. Verlag, Volume 1.)

Now let us compare what is written in the same source about the half-halt:

> Half-halts are used to:
> – bring the horse into a lower gait,
> – shorten the gait,
> – improve collection and carriage,
> – call the horse's attention to a new exercise,
> – regain lost carriage,
> – obtain flexion,
> – counteract pressing on the bit and a gait that is too fast.
> With active leg aids and a braced back the rider provides sufficient rein by rounding the wrist. At the first suggestion of response, the

rein should be released. If necessary, these aids may be repeated
several times. The rider uses the reins in such a way that they never
operate rearward, but rather so that the horse steps into them. The
often heard phrase "half-halt on the left or right, or outside rein" is
misleading, because it sounds as if the half-halt consists only of
taking up the correct rein. It is, however, the driving aids that are
most important, and without them the half-halt is impossible. The half-
halt as described above can only be correctly executed when the hind
legs are drawn up and consciously driven forward for a short instant
on both reins (straight lines), or on the outside rein (curved lines). In
summary, the half-halt is executed by means of momentarily restricting the horse — using leg, weight, and rein aids — followed by releasing the rein.

Anyone with any riding experience will have good reason to doubt
that the same aids (as described above in the definition of a half-halt)
can bring a horse, for instance, from a medium canter to a working
canter, from a working canter to a working trot, from a working canter
to a walk, or from a working trot to a walk, just because each of these
brings the horse to a lower gait.

Four *different* aids are necessary for each of those four examples.
And these four procedures cannot be dispensed with by maintaining
that a half-halt will do it all.

Nor can you both use the same half-halt to obtain collection and
flexion, because in collection we want the horse to place its weight on
its hind legs and in flexion we use the inside leg and inside rein to ask
for a flexing of the lower jaw. Neither of these procedures has anything
at all to do with the other. The training instructions quoted earlier are
too simplified; thus, one of the most important teaching procedures in
riding is handled summarily in a very unclear fashion.

In his very noteworthy book, *Vollendete Reitkunst,* Udo Bürger
writes:

> We would give our students a better understanding of handling the
> reins in conjunction with gait if we spoke not only of half-halt and
> complete halt, but of quarter- and tenth-halts. For the horse in training
> and for the student rider, a halt should be broken up into many care-
> fully applied small halts. (Bürger, U. 1975: *Vollendete Reitkunst,* 3rd
> ed. Berlin and Hamburg: Paul Parey.)

In the annals of equestrian history, the halt formerly sought only the
bending of the hind legs; halts, in their multiplicity, were once regarded
as the crowning achievement of dressage carriage. Trainers initially

exercised only one of a young horse's hind legs (on the arc of a circle, the inside leg). They drew each hind leg *individually* under the center of gravity, putting weight on it and flexing it. This activity was formerly called a "half-halt."

When both hind legs were sufficiently developed that weight could be shifted to *both* of them together and distributed evenly, this was called a "complete" halt. The complete halt was used first to collect and later to bring the horse to a halt. Thus, in earlier parlance, a half-halt referred to shifting weight to one hind leg, whereas a complete halt involved shifting weight to both hind legs.

The excellent book, *Gymnasium des Pferdes,* which presents the historical development of the above described halt, also contains this momentous statement:

> Thus we must reexamine and correct the current thinking on the difference between the half-halt and the complete halt which holds that the complete halt brings the horse to a stop while the half-halt only causes it to shorten its gait or to gather itself, i.e., to collect itself. (Steinbrecht, G. 1978: *Gymnasium des Pferdes,* 10th ed. Aachen: Dr. R. Georgi.)

Considering that the first edition of *Gymnasium des Pferdes* appeared in 1884, it is amazing that over 100 years later still nothing has been done to correct the thinking about halts. Training for utilitarian military purposes no doubt led to a simple rule of thumb for the cavalry drill book: half-halts and complete halts. After all, cavalry troop training did not include shoulder in or collected gaits, nor did it teach pirouettes or half-passes.

However, for our purposes, we should know something more than this rather obtuse equation for the half-halt. For this reason, I have delved into the historical development of the halt even though it goes beyond the scope of this book.

After this introduction to the section on halt, I shall return to the training of your young horse. However, from now on, based on the considerations set forth above, I shall no longer use the terms "complete halt" and "half-halt."

Aids for halting

The basis of the halt is a braced spine, not to be confused with throwing yourself back. Previous sections, for example, "Lengthening and

Shortening" and "Developing the Canter," already addressed bracing the back and tensing the spine.

• *Remember*: The halt is not possible without using your back.

The next question is *how much* exertion from the back is required for each type of halt. The answer is as much as necessary, and that depends upon the horse's level of training, its day-to-day fluctuations, and its current degree of throughness. Thus, for example, a horse may totally ignore the back aids at the beginning of the riding lesson, whereas at the end of the lesson he responds to a slight bracing of the seat. This is an indication that the lesson has gone well.

In addition to bracing the back, of course, other aids are necessary to execute a halt, namely leg, weight, and rein. To perform a promising halt we must understand the exact effects of these aids. The *leg* exerts a driving effect on the horse's hind leg of the same side, driving *forward* when positioned *on* the girth, and driving *sideward* when positioned *behind* the girth. In other words, the leg aids direct the horse's hind legs. The rider's *weight* guides the horse forward or sideward (horizontal effect); however, you can also shift your weight more to the forelegs or the hind legs (vertical effect). The *rein* has a checking effect on the pair of legs on the same side as the respective rein. When bending do not forget that the bending rein also has a simultaneous checking effect; consequently, when turning you must always activate the inside hind leg with your inside leg aid. The reins direct the forelegs. If you understand and have mastered the effects of leg, weight, and rein, you will always be able to execute a correct halt.

It is not the purpose of this book to present "halt combinations" for individual transitions, because, as has been repeatedly emphasized, only a genuinely experienced trainer can break in a young horse and encourage its further development. Just two examples should demonstrate the contrast between the effects (both are called "half-halt").

Example One: Transition from canter to trot. The inside hand that has been letting up at each canter stride draws back *against the stride* once, thereby checking the inside legs from further forward motion. At the same instant, brace your back, move your leg from behind the girth to the girth, and increase the pressure of the inside seat bone, thus returning to a normal seat. If despite these aids your horse continues to canter, then repeat the procedure. And I repeat: Bracing the back is the most important factor.

Example Two: Transition from medium canter to working canter.
Since the horse is supposed to continue cantering, you must remain in
canter seat and continue to let the stride out with the inside hand. The
actual shortening of the stride is achieved with your back and outside
hand at the moment the horse sets down its inside foreleg. Your inside
leg must keep driving the horse's inside hind leg firmly so that he does
not fall into a trot. The inside spur may also be used for additional
support.

The following recommendations will make the halt comprehensible
to your young horse. Ride the entire arena at a walk. Your horse must
be firmly on the bit, and you must have a completely steady seat. Now
slowly brace your back pulling your spine upward (slight tensing of the
back muscles) and at the same time step deeper into both stirrups with
lowered heel until your horse comes to a stop. Keep a motionless seat,
even after stopping (don't look down, don't try to adjust your seat,
don't wipe your nose). Now *touch* the horse lightly with both legs so
that it steps out again.

This exercise is the basis for the halt. In executing it, endeavor to do
nothing with your hands; initially, it might be necessary to close the
hands slightly (as if squeezing a sponge), but the goal is to get by
without use of your hands.

When the horse understands this lesson, go to the next step — transition between trot and walk — with the same slight back action. During
this exercise do not forget change of hand or the transition between the
whole arena and the circle. However, always line up the horse *straight*
on the *circle* before the halt.

The next stage is the transition between trot and halt. Our lesson to
the horse is very clear — leg means trot, back means stop. Put your
horse into a brisk working trot, brace your back upward, and at the
same time step into both stirrups. The horse will stop, and you will
have achieved this without hand action. This is the consummate halt to
full-stop. You will discover a beautiful by-product: the horse is suddenly standing nicely balanced on all four legs, like a picture-book
pose.

Always forewarn the horse with a suggestion from your fingertips
that you are going to halt to a full-stop; you never want to take the
horse completely by surprise with this maneuver. Keep in mind, too,
that a halt should never be too hard; hard halts ruin the fetlocks.
Furthermore, never look down after stopping, or worse yet, try to

correct the foot positioning. A well-balanced horse that has been introduced to the halt properly will stand correctly on its own. If it does not,
be patient and continue with basic training.

- *Remember*:   A successful halt to full-stop followed by
  standing quietly is an impressive achievement.

Before each new lesson, imply a halt (slight, almost invisible bracing of the back), especially before changing from one lead to the other,
or, when riding a serpentine across the arena, each time you cross the
center line.

Before each halt, it is very important to call the hind legs forward
with the leg aids. After the halt, leave your leg resting on the horse so
that he does not step backward. Moreover, after coming to a full-stop,
your hand must slightly moderate the tension to your horse's mouth.
Standing still is a lesson that many riders do not consider worth practicing and they often pay very dearly for this later.

The back is, of course, required for the success of all halts. In
addition, though, the upper arms, positioned vertically against the
body, must be absolutely steady. Never draw the reins back with your
arms; instead curl your wrists in, or better yet, close your hands.

The more weight that can be shifted to the hind legs in the halt, the
better the halt will be. The prerequisite for this, however, is months of
basic training for the horse. The journey from the first attempt to check
a young horse with the rein to the consummate halt is long, often very
long. Thus at the beginning of training we do not even consider teaching a halt. You cannot undertake the halt or begin to work on throughness until the horse stands steadily on the rein, has strong drive from
the hind legs, and a supple back. A full-stop, when a horse with good
elevation is standing absolutely still, presents a picture of controlled
strength and beauty.

Medium trot

The foundation for the medium trot was introduced in the section on
"Drive and Initial Elevation" under the heading "Lengthening and
Shortening the Trot." The concepts of "drive" and "impulsion" are also
discussed there. The development of a medium trot actually comes
from letting the horse step out from a shortened working trot on the
long wall.

The aids are as follows: The head is held high. The shoulders, elbows, and hands are kept low. The outside hand, in particular, is held somewhat lower than the right. The inside hand lets up on the stride (the horse should reach the inside rein), but under no circumstances should the rein be slack. A deep seat is required from which you will push the horse with both legs. The horse must move forward freely, but firmly on the outside rein under comfortable tension, and the hind legs must develop energetic drive. The horse is clearly more on the rein than at a working trot. The shortening occurs with the back aid opposing the somewhat higher positioned hand, while the leg aid simultaneously draws the hind legs forward so they can carry more weight.

At first, ask for only a few strides, and then repeat this twice on the long wall (step out — shorten — step out — shorten). Later you can also practice stepping out on the diagonal and then on the short wall.

In developing the medium trot, the rider must sit very straight so that the horse does not go into a canter. Therefore, do not let your horse step out right out of the corner, but straighten him first. This is especially true for stepping out on the diagonal. The extended trot is developed only on straight lines. When you ride the entire arena later, be sure to round off the corners well. The same is true for the medium canter.

A lifeless, dragging working trot will never develop into a medium trot; to step out, the horse needs a certain excitement (not tenseness). Lazy horses should be perked up before starting; the rider must have the feeling that his horse is virtually waiting to step out.

Ideally, teach your horse the medium trot as follows:

(a) Transition between working trot and slow trot.
(b) Let the horse step out to the medium trot from a slow trot on the long wall, but only for a few strides.
(c) Step out twice on the long wall.
(d) Development on the diagonal.
(e) Let the horse step out on the long wall, but don't demand "everything" yet; ride the whole arena and extend again on the next long side.

In developing the medium trot, just as throughout the rest of training, build from the bottom, always seeking to set limits so that errors in rhythm do not creep in. Under no circumstances should you let the horse fall apart. With nervous horses do not practice too many tempo changes; however, you can use them to liven up a phlegmatic, placid horse. Keep in mind that the pace sequence should never get faster in the medium trot; extension means nothing more than taking longer strides with more impulsion. The noseline must be clearly in front of the vertical.

Frequent transitions between medium trot and slow trot for the rest of the horse's education are an excellent exercise to increase the elasticity of the horse's hind legs. Preferably, ride a volte at a slow trot in the first corner of the long side, straighten out, and let the horse step out.

Some horses learn the medium trot without much effort; others will require considerable work. In this case, the rule is to take your time and strengthen the hind legs. Never pound with your legs, lean backward, or let yourself be carried away by the horse; instead go with the movement maintaining a deep seat with hips forward.

Never demand too much from the horse. When tired, he will not have enough energy, and often he will forge. Forging results when a tired horse becomes front-heavy and the forelegs leave the ground a fraction of a second too late catching the tips of the hind hoofs.

Horses that forge must be positioned more on their hind legs; this is also true of young horses being broken. In such cases, do not trot with a light seat — i.e., do not go into a rising trot but go to a sitting trot after a substantial amount of work at walk.

Cavaletti work and gymnastic jumping

At the very latest by the end of basic training you should start working with low obstacles. Obstacle work promotes the gaits taught in basic training. Indeed, cavaletti work is an excellent aid for horses with stiff backs. Remember that all training in jumping begins with cavaletti exercises and then moves on to more advanced jumping.

It would go beyond the purpose of this book to detail exercises with low obstacles and jumping training, but I can recommend several very good German books on the subject: Klimke, R. *Cavaletti.* 6th ed. Stuttgart: Franckh'sche Verlagshandlung; Paalman, A. 1986: *Spring-Reiten,* 6th ed. Stuttgart: Franckh'sche Verlagshandlung; Thiedemann, F. 1979: *Das Springpferd.* Edition Haberbek. All three books contain worthwhile recommendations for cavaletti work and the two latter books are excellent reference works on jumping.

Closing thoughts on Part One

Basic training should be considered complete with the lesson on the medium trot. Note the emphasis on the word "basic." I assume that your young horse spent the summer of his third year on the meadow, that he began longeing that winter after being stalled, that his saddle training began when he was four, and that he is now five. At this point you must allow at least one year for basic training with a rider. It would be even better to allow *more* time.

At the conclusion of basic training the horse has been introduced to all the lessons needed for the low level dressage tests, which is not to say that the horse is necessarily ready to *take* the tests.

The criteria for low level dressage are as follows:

1. Special attention is given to the footfall sequence of the three basic gaits;
2. Suppleness of horse's back and rider's seat;
3. Natural forward movement and light contact in a working posture;
4. Noticeable throughness in halts;
5. Beginning bending work, with neck steady at the shoulder;
6. Obedience to both the forward-driving *and* lateral leg aids;
7. Stands quietly at a halt, though a *slight* adjustment in footing is not judged to be a major fault.

You may have noticed that the listed criteria make no mention of lessons and school figures. This is because the lessons are not the primary purpose of the dressage test, but rather the means to an end by which the listed criteria can be tested. Thus, a correctly ridden simple serpentine is of no value if the horse is not flexed correctly, if he is behind the vertical, or if he goes on two tracks. Many inexperienced riders practice dressage figures superficially without having the slightest comprehension of what is really required.

An old rule states that when a horse is ready for a given level of dressage, then start him at the level just below. In your case your young horse belongs in a lowest level test, if any at all. Without setting up a rigid time schedule, we can safely say that a horse that is broken at four years old belongs in a lowest level test no earlier than the age of five and in a next level test not before six years old. If we hold to this rule, we would spare both spectators at competitions and ourselves many graceless performances!

Unfortunately, many horses never reach a competition level, because they have been trained by riders who have overestimated their own abilities and are convinced that they can train without the help or advice of an expert. It is easy to spot riders with this over-inflated opinion of themselves. When working with their horses they keep the upper part of their bodies bent forward as they desperately practice pirouettes, try to collect on the rein, or even attempt a flying change. Don't they know how ridiculous they look? Impulsion and rhythm have long since been abandoned.

Lest there be misunderstanding, it is recommended that *every* young horse, including future jumpers and three-day eventers, complete basic training up to low level dressage. Even the person who just likes to go hacking would be well-advised to have a qualified trainer bring his horse to this point. This training will not only make riding more fun, but it is particularly important for the health of rider and horse, as well as anyone else who comes in contact with them.

Part Two

5

Collection work and beyond

In bygone days when the training of young horses was divided into the training of "young remounts" and "old remounts," the education of old remounts began the second year after first breaking them in. The horses were worked daily. Without wanting to establish a strict schedule, I would like to emphasize that today we should allow at least one or two years of basic before beginning with collection proper. Collection is only possible after the hindquarters have been sufficiently exercised and strengthened by means of logically developed basic training.

At the conclusion of basic training, the horse should always move in a working posture. The work that follows aims to improve contact, straightness, and throughness. A further prerequisite for collection is an impeccable seat on the part of the rider, which requires many years of intensive training.

Defining collection

More correctly, collection should be termed "collection on the hind-quarters." The mutual center of gravity of both horse and rider is shifted more to the rear; thus, the horse carries more weight with its hind legs and less with its forelegs. As a result, the horse is more elevated in front (relative lifting of the head), it carries its neck and head higher, and its stride becomes more elevated, but shorter. Purity of gaits, however, must be preserved and impulsion encouraged.

How to collect the horse

Collection is achieved in two ways: from the seat and with appropriate exercises.

Collection from the seat can be demonstrated with the illustration of a wooden rocking horse that you do not want to rock but to stay still (Figure 5). When, in addition to shifting your weight, you use both legs to push the horse's hind legs under the center of gravity, then the back heaviness created by the seat is intensified. The horse is forced to increase the bending of hip and stifle joints (bending the haunches), and the bent haunches take on more weight (Figure 6). This then brings us to the next stage.

Collection with appropriate exercises. In all the training that follows there is a common element connecting theory and practice. This element is the hindquarters. As the old riders' adage goes: Master the hindquarters and you have mastered the horse. All efforts at collection must strive for three goals: narrow hind leg tracks, flexing the haunches, impulsion.

Collection is impossible without narrow tracks. The wider apart the horse's hind legs are, the less collected it is. With no help from the rider, a horse with a straightened spine will proceed on the long wall in such a way that its outside pair of legs will follow in the same track, but the inside hind leg will land somewhat more to the inside, next to the track of the inner foreleg. (See also the discussion of straightening in the section on "Flexion, Bend, and Angle.")

In collection we must always bring the inside hind leg into the track of the inside foreleg. Leg aids on both sides ensure that the horse's hind legs move close to one another and are set down as close to the midsection of the horse's body as possible. The strength of the hind legs can not be properly engaged without this narrow track. The rider must create a frame around the horse. In other words, the rider's leg aids guide the horse's hind legs.

Bending the haunches

The real strength of the hindquarters comes from the haunches. With the haunches flexed, the hind legs must take on more weight and carry the added weight elastically, but also push off with more power. Earlier sections have already stressed that work on a circle is extremely impor-

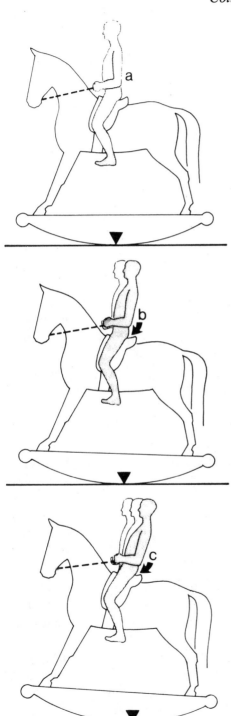

Figure 5. (a) Normal seat; rider's spine at a right angle to the horse's back. (b) Light collection; bracing the seat upwards and rearwards, while at the same time pushing the lower half of the spine forward. The horse is more on the back of the rockers.

(c) High collection; shift of weight increased, horse even lower in the rear and higher in front.

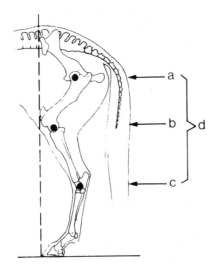

Figure 6. (a) Hip joint.
(b) Stifle Joint. (c) Hock.
(d) Haunch.

tant for bending the haunches, because it exercises each inside hind leg particularly well. Increasing and decreasing the size of the circle at a slow trot or at a collected trot is a lesson that is, unfortunately, often neglected despite its great utility. Antique prints clearly illustrate what "bending the haunches" meant to riding masters of the past.

Impulsion

Driving action from the hindquarters is the preliminary stage for impulsion. However, in young horses this driving action comes more from the wide-tracked steps of the hind legs. When the rider refines this natural driving action by introducing flexed haunches and a narrow track, then we have *impulsion*. From impulsion comes an elevated forehand. However, a horse must have a relaxed, supple back to develop impulsion.

In this initial phase of collection it would be a great mistake to try to achieve collection and elevation with the *rein*, because the hind legs cannot yet accept the weight that is forced back with the hand. The result would be spiritless, dragging steps and a stiff back. According to the classical rule, the horse must always be collected from back to front, against a somewhat more elevated hand, which, however, never pulls back. In applying collection aids, the legs always come first, calling the horse's hind legs forward. Then comes the seat, which shifts more weight to the hind legs. Last comes the rein, to restrict and possibly to help flex. Thus, collection results when the impulsion from the hind legs on a narrow track is so transformed by an immobile hand that the haunches flex and the forehand rises.

For all collected gaits keep in mind that it is better to sacrifice carriage than forward impulsion. Finally, despite the need for a certain amount of book knowledge, the process of collection cannot be understood purely in theoretical terms. Experience and what the rider feels are paramount!

Collected trot

In the lessons on "Lengthening and Shortening," the horse was already taught the difference between driving and carrying. The collected trot is developed by shortening the medium trot. The rider braces upward and rearward against the slightly higher hand on a short rein. (The rein and the forearm should, however, now form a straight line.)

When the haunches are bent, the hind legs carry more weight, the load on the forehand is eased, and the forehand is elevated. Both legs, possibly with the aid of spurs, are responsible for maintaining forward impulsion; there should be no lagging. Without impulsion there is no elevation; this is a simple statement that, despite the truth of it, many fail to comprehend. For instance, many try to lift their horses from the front by hand.

- *Remember*: Collected gaits require impulsion.

In collection, it is also especially important to build cautiously and to increase demands slowly. Work at the collected trot for short stretches only, and then always follow this exercise with free gaits. Do not keep the horse's neck too short. The noseline should never be behind the vertical. In the free paces allow the horse a slightly extended posture.

Stroke the horse occasionally during collecting exercises to check whether it is in self-carriage or leaning on the rein. (Move your rein hand well forward to the crest, running your hand over the mane stroking slowly back down.)

If the horse goes too low or seems heavy on the forehand, the higher hand must force it upward vigorously. If this is not effective, press up with the seat and the inside spur against the *outside* hand—never against the inside hand. Work in collected trot will gradually transform normal carriage into the *dressage carriage* that is necessary for further training.

- *Remember:* If the trot becomes listless, use the canter to enliven it.

Collected canter

Before you can begin training to develop a collected canter, the horse must have adequate self-carriage in the medium canter. As was the case with the collected trot, build up to it carefully. Undue haste will only cause damage. The collected canter demands even more intense flexing of the haunches than was necessary in the collected trot. Thus, it would not be wise to expect an impeccable collected canter from your average horse; only horses with better than average talent for dressage and excellent bending in the hindquarters can progress to the collected canter of the more advanced levels of dressage.

The collected canter is learned on a circle by repeatedly practicing the transition to a canter from a collected trot and later from a walk. Canter for only short stretches at a time. The horse does not learn the collected canter by actual cantering, but rather by frequent transitions to and from a canter using half-halts. Only the *first* strides of each of these exercises promote the collected canter. If a horse ceases to carry itself correctly, then it is necessary to halt at once.

In the collected canter, the rider must take a deep seat and step deeply into the inside stirrup as if he wanted to break the stirrup leather. If your horse moves too fast, regulate it with your back and short movement of the *outside* rein at the moment the horse sets down his inside foreleg. Teaching a horse the collected canter requires considerable time and great skill on the part of the rider. At the highest level, we practice cantering from the rein back, where, with sharp bending of the hips, stifles, and hocks, the horse must thrust its hind legs under its center of gravity like a taut spring.

It is a grave error to demand the collected canter prematurely. The result can be strides that lack impulsion, a stiff back, head tossing, and, particularly, two-track cantering. Cantering on two tracks is a considerable problem for many riders, especially on the right lead where many horses place their hind legs to the inside. In this case a slight shoulder in (often more implied than executed) helps to correct the fault. In this connection especially, refer back to the section in Part I on "Flexion, Bend, Angle" in which straightening is discussed in more detail.

- *Remember*: The collected canter should always feel like an uphill canter in triple time.

Counter canter

Within the space limitations of this book riding in counter-flexion can only be treated peripherally and summarily, because these lessons are not part of basic training. (By riding in flexion or "counter-flexion" we mean with bending of the entire spine.)

Many riders are unfamiliar with riding in flexion to the outside and many instructors leave it out. However, counter exercises at a collected trot demand a very high degree of concentration, throughness, and responsiveness from a horse. Moreover, it is a good way to correct horses who push into the track with the forehand. In addition, flexion to the outside can be used to eliminate the nasty habit of pressing against the wall, a vice common to many horses. Above all, riding in flexion to the outside serves as preparation for counter canter and side steps.

Initially, training begins at a walk around the arena with slight lower jaw flexion to the outside; corners are ridden in the same fashion (but somewhat rounded off). Next go around the large circle. Gradually attempt to achieve outside bending of the *entire* spine. Once outside bending is stabilized at a walk, repeat the same exercises at a trot. You must use your knee to keep the concave side of the horse on the line of the circle. Avoid pulling the horse's neck around; and note that, even in flexion to the outside, the neck should not be bent *more* than the rest of the spinal column.

Practice first only on one lead in order to stabilize flexion to the outside. When that has been achieved, ride the whole arena, cantering so that the horse goes into a counter canter at about the point where the first circle intersects the long side of the arena.

A correctly schooled and well-prepared horse will move effortlessly into a counter canter. It is important to remain correctly seated without moving (step into the stirrup on the concave side of the horse) and round off the next corner. After that, it is time to execute a half-halt and praise your horse — don't forget to let it stretch. Work only on one lead, leaving the other lead for the next day. Your horse should be given a chance to mentally digest the new lesson first.

It is important to note that all exercises for counter-flexion fall under the rubric of *collection*, requiring a horse that is secure in a collected trot and collected canter. This is particularly true because in the beginning horses tend to become front-heavy when working in flexion to the outside, and they try to avoid collection. In addition, remember that a rider in counter-flexion — as in all bending lessons — must in general sit a little lower on the concave side, that is with a lowered inside knee, but without bending at the hip.

A further exercise to teach the horse the counter canter is the half circle with change of rein from the second corner on the long side without a canter change. Round off the next two corners on the short side and immediately change back to the true canter on the long wall. Do not allow your horse to become excited while working on the counter canter. Give it frequent breaks to rest and stretch. (The counter canter is dealt with extensively in: Knopfhart, A. 1987: *Dressur von A-S,* 2nd ed. Berlin and Hamburg: Paul Parey.)

- *Remember*: When riding counter canter, do not interfere or coerce — sit quietly and go with the movement.

Rein back

The rein back is a collecting exercise requiring a horse that is completely responsive to the aids and absolutely through. At higher levels of dressage, the rein back aims toward increased bending of the haunches, thus resulting in better collection. However, because it is a movement that goes against the horse's nature, it must not be introduced too early and all use of force must be avoided.

In the case of a young horse in the first stage of basic training, the rein back consists more of shuffling or creeping back. The aids for this are to hold the hands low, to alternate rein movement from one side to the other, and to slightly lessen pressure from the seat. In advanced dressage schooling, the rider remains seated with his back braced slightly and presses the horse, which is standing next to the wall, gently backward with the inside leg. If there is no wall, then he applies the backward aids with both legs. The wrists are slightly curled. In addition, the somewhat retracted inside leg prevents the hind legs from moving in. The horse must never be *pulled* backward with the rein; a well-schooled horse under the aids should step back without an active rein.

As already mentioned, not only must the horse be responsive to the aids prior to reining back, but it must remain so during the process. It should step calmly and willingly rearward on a straight line, lifting its diagonal legs, not rushing or dragging them.

Very important for the success of the rein back is the preceding transition to a full-stop with hind legs nicely placed under the center of gravity. After stepping backward the horse must also stand correctly and quietly again.

One recommended exercise — especially to develop bending of the haunches — is that of going into a collected trot from rein back. For both of these movements, the diagonal sequence of steps (two-beat rhythm) is helpful. If a horse refuses to step backward, you must work on throughness first. Half-halts with a change of tempo at a trot are particularly helpful. If your horse pushes against the wall with its hind legs during the rein back (a rather common fault), it often is an indication that you are sitting too much to the inside. An erect seat with the inside leg noticeably drawn back usually helps; if this doesn't work, give the horse an implied shoulder in while stepping back (but without sitting toward the inside).

Spurs

Spurs are necessary for collection, thus we must concern ourselves with this dressage aid. Some riders reject spurs as a matter of principle, while others are of the opinion that spurs, like the whip, are necessary riding equipment. Lest there be misunderstanding, though, *only* riders with an impeccable seat, low heels, and steady legs should wear spurs. This is especially true in training young horses. In the first year of basic training, try to get by without spurs.

The purpose of spurs is to assist your legs, not substitute for them. Thus, spurs should only be employed if a horse does not respond to leg aids, and then only in *conjunction* with leg aids. A good rider knows how to distinguish between *putting on* the spurs (letting them be felt), *pressing* with the spurs, and *jabbing* with the spurs. The greatest mistake with spurs is using them with the heels drawn up to drive the horse forward. It is the task of the leg to call forward the horse's hind leg on the same side. In the case of lazy horses, just putting on the spurs as a continuation of leg pressure is usually sufficient assistance. Jabbing, on the other hand, calls the hind leg upward, away from the ground.

- *Remember*: The leg drives — the spur collects.

We are dependent on the help of spurs when we want to go from a medium canter to a working canter or even to a collected canter. Here, while stepping firmly into the inside stirrup, we use the spur to keep the inside hind leg active.

There are exceptions when a jab with the spur can also be used as punishment, for example, with nappy horses. In this case, however, give them a jab *in front of* the girth in order to prevent them from kicking. The rider should also consider that a nappy horse may not be on the aids, in which case *this* is where the fault should be corrected. Spurs should be used as punishment only in the most extreme circumstances. Never punish a horse in anger (especially a young horse), because an unjustly administered jab of the spur damages the relationship of trust between horse and rider. All spur aids should be independent of the seat. There is an interesting reflection by Udo Bürger on the use of spurs in his book *Vollendete Reitkunst*. (Bürger. U. 1982: *Vollendete Reitkunst*, 5th ed. Berlin and Hamburg: Paul Parey). There he notes:

> Spurs are an extension of the lower leg designed to strengthen or refine the leg's action. Before strapping on the spurs, one should give some thought to how one wants to use them. To drive, to punish, to collect, or to mold the gait? The first two uses are primitive and are on the same level as using a whip on young or unbroken horses. The spurs are only a reinforcement of leg action that should also be effective without them.
>
> The collecting and simultaneous checking action of the spurs, on the other hand, is a refinement of the leg movement and is thus a sensitive matter. The precise, alternating assistance of the spur as a prick at the girth in connection with half-halts brings the change from shortened steps into collection and beyond into noble school airs. . .
>
> It may sound paradoxical to attribute a checking action to the spurs, but the transition between passage and trot is scarcely possible any other way; passage with alternating spurs, and the signal to trot given by the leg.
>
> The use of spurs requires practice. The correct feeling is obtained wearing jodhpurs and placing the spurs over the edge of your ankle

boots so that they lie directly on the sock covering your heel tendon. Thus any violent action is automatically precluded. Use only pointed or sharp-edged spurs. Round, buttonlike imitations and small wheels have an unpredictable effect and can confuse the horse. Small wheels that tear can be instruments of torture.

Used correctly, each spur enlivens a hind leg and nothing more. If you comprehend this, you will never again use both spurs simultaneously because the prick of the spur on the side of the forward-moving hind leg would induce collection, while on the other side it would induce speed in the hind leg that is pushing off. This does nothing but confuse the horse.

For simple driving you do not prick with the spurs, but merely exert pressure; and as mentioned above, in time even this becomes superfluous. For example, to teach a young horse the transition from trot to canter, move your outside leg toward the rear while exerting firm pressure at the girth with the inside leg, first using the upper edge of the boot leg, then with the entire calf, and if the horse still does not canter, use the spur together with the whip. Let up on the aids the moment the horse canters. If this procedure is repeated often enough with precision, the horse will no longer wait for the pressure of the spurs and whip, but will react appropriately to the pressure of the upper edge of the boot leg. The principle is always the same: Refine the aids systematically.

• *Remember*: The better the rider, the less spur he needs.

Ready for the curb

Some riders feel they are ready for the curb bit the moment they get their bronze. In many cases then, the curb bit is used to bluff one's way into a higher dressage level. Very often the double bridle is used as a more refined substitute for a running rein by riders who are unable to put their horses to the aids while on the snaffle bit. There are even riders who believe that this is the real purpose of the curb bit. A horse that is abused in this way will either lose all impulsion or begin to rear. Real readiness for the curb bit, on the part of horses as well as their riders, is rarer than you think.

A young horse is ready for the curb bit when it has worked its way through the patient and exacting training described above, and when it performs collection exercises on the snaffle bit with confident self-carriage and superior throughness. The curb bit is intended to refine the

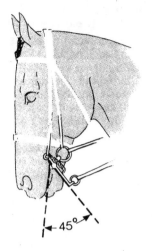

Figure 7. Correctly adjusted curb chain.

carriage that has been acquired on the snaffle bit. Consideration must be given to the leverlike effect of the curb, which intensifies the force of the rider's hand many times over.

In order to accustom the horse to the unfamiliar double bridle, the curb chain is only loosely adjusted at the start and the curb rein is not taken up at this time. The horse should get accustomed to the new bridling on long, straight lines at first. Once that has been accomplished, the curb chain is adjusted properly and the same kind of training is repeated — possibly for a shorter period of time. (The curb chain is properly adjusted when the cheeks are at a forty-five degree angle to the mouth aperture when the reins are tightened. See Figure 7.)

Initially, collection exercises should not be performed using a double bridle, because the horse must first learn to step trustingly into the lightly *elastic* curb bit. Stepping up to the bit without fear and with some impulsion is the touchstone for further training. Only when the gait maintains impulsion can the actual work of refining collection begin.

Horses who are ready for the curb bit must, however, be worked again from time to time on the snaffle, especially if they develop clamped lower jaws. Exact flexing of the lower jaw is only possible on the snaffle bit, because the curb bit allows almost no one-sided bending. Thus, work with the snaffle bit must provide a basis for lower jaw bending, even in advanced stages of training.

In bending with the double bridle, the inside snaffle rein introduces the bending, the outside curb rein releases. Later the horse will also learn the restricting and guiding functions of the outside curb rein. Initially the outside curb rein should not be too short, and the rein must be corrected and rearranged at every change of hand.

In working with the curb bit, one thing is especially important and cannot be overemphasized, and that is that the hind legs must step firmly under the weight of the horse (under the center of gravity) in a narrow track. As soon as the hind legs go wide or start to drag, the rider is on the wrong track.

In concluding this chapter, the writer asks the following question: How many riders use a double bridle but have never concerned themselves with the questions and concerns discussed here? Many, probably very many, and these riders are not ready for the curb bit. Remember again the adage: Dressage is not an end in itself, but a means to an end. It is intensive, painstaking work. The heights of success are few and far between, but they do exist, and usually they are unforgettable, for instance the first feeling of suppleness and a relaxed back. Many years go by before you comprehend what it means "to canter to a halt." Suddenly, after years of riding, you discover and feel what you have sought for so long but only read about in books. These moments are the zenith of horsemanship.

Closing thoughts on Part Two

The path we have described, taking the horse from young, green mount to one ready for the curb bit, demonstrates the individual stages of schooling according to the guidelines and experience of the classical art of equitation. The Greek, Xenophon (fourth century B.C.), laid the cornerstone for today's equitation. The names Guérinière and Caprilli are famous in the history of riding, and great men like Seeger, Steinbrecht, Bürkner, to mention just a few, have brought worldwide recognition to the German style of equitation.

They are reason enough to adhere to time-tested principles of the past in training young horses. These are the golden rules of riding:

- Ride your horse forward and point it straight.
- Never punish in anger.
- Boredom is the enemy of learning. Always allow for free paces after collected gaits.
- Sacrifice carriage rather than forward impulsion.

- Offer frequent opportunities to stretch and relax at walk on a long rein.
- Never demand too much of a young horse.
- Only a few ever master the art of ending a lesson at exactly the right moment.
- Praise too much rather than too little.
- Don't look for short cuts in dressage.

Some topics in this book have had to be treated briefly and limited only to essentials. On the one hand, this gives the reader the advantage of not having to pore through endless pages of learned dissertation. On the other hand, many issues are left open, e.g., problem horses, vices, horses with physical or character defects. In many instances, however, these are horses that have been broken incorrectly, and it is not the task of this book to give instruction or recommendations about retraining.

If, during training, irreconcilable and irremediable physical and character defects appear in your horse which even an experienced rider cannot correct or which can be corrected only with great effort, you should get rid of the horse. Often such a horse can look forward to a long and pleasant life as a family pet or hacking horse.

Some other subjects that do not actually belong to basic training, but are very important for the horse owner, are presented and discussed in Part Three.

Part Three

6

Further topics — unanswered questions

What is the difference between leg yielding and shoulder in?

Leg yielding

Leg yielding is a *suppling* exercise. With it the horse should first of all become familiar with the one-sided laterally driving leg, and in the course of further training then discover the limiting (opposing) outside leg. The horse must be straightened in the spine and move out with *slight* flexing of the lower jaw. The angle from the wall should not exceed forty-five degrees. Leg yielding should be practiced sparingly. (See also "Suppling Exercises," Part 1.)

Shoulder in

Shoulder in is a collecting exercise and the basis for all lateral movement; it is not a basic training exercise. The absolute prerequisites for shoulder in are throughness, collection, and elevation. In this exercise the horse moves with obvious longitudinal bending. While the hind legs move straight forward, the forehand is about half a step off the track as a result of the bending. In other words, the inside hind leg steps in the direction of the outside foreleg (see Figure 8).

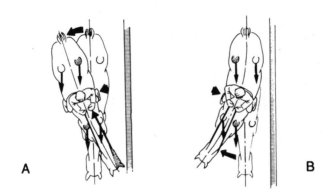

Figure 8. (a) Leg yielding: spine straight, slight flexing of lower jaw. (b) Shoulder in, horse bent. (Knopfhart, 1988.)

Cool down in the saddle or on the lead?

Young horses often sweat more from excitement than from exertion. Because dismounting after a workout represents a reward for the horse, you should dismount and *walk* the horse until he is dry rather than riding him dry. Riders demonstrate little consideration as equestrians when they, as they so often do, ride their mounts dry in pairs around the arena, chattering with their companions, thereby disturbing the work of other riders.

In the winter, wet horses should be covered and led dry in the ring while in summer this can be done outdoors in the sun. In either case, look for an area free of drafts. Wet, sweaty horses should not be taken back to the stall. Horses with winter coats should not be ridden into a sweat. For instance, during the winter do not schedule canter work at the end of the lesson.

While we are on the subject of leading, always walk on the left side of the horse; when turning, always go to the right, thereby pushing the horse away from you (except when leading a lame horse).

Wrong bend in the neck

Putting the horse to the aids is the result of pressure against the passive hand, suppleness, and lower jaw sensitivity. A horse on the rein should always be reaching for the ground, with its poll the highest point. In this position, the noseline is in front of the vertical. Despite sensitivity and suppleness, the rider should always feel definite forward contact. The oft heard statement "My horse is moving well—I don't have anything in my hand anymore" reveals that this contact has been lost. Usually, the result is that the horse tips behind the vertical, compresses itself, and is no longer on the aids. The only thing that will help in this case is *riding forward vigorously* using the whip. Under no circumstances should you pull back on the reins. Instead, release them to the front so that the horse can again reach for the ground.

Horses that always get behind the vertical or whose riders even work them in this carriage, develop a "wrong bend," that is, a bend in the neck between the second and third vertebrae. This rather unattractive head set precludes lowering the hindquarters, raising the head, or developing free gaits. The worst, however, is that such horses are no longer on the aids and consequently are not obedient at critical moments.

The equestrian dream: flying changes

In the imagination of every rider, from novice to the most advanced, there is a progression of milestones, starting more or less with spurs, and proceeding to a private horse, curb bit, top hat, and culminating in the flying change. Every one of these dreams can be purchased with one exception: the flying change at a canter which the rider must truly earn.

Take a look at a riding school. When a poor rider wants to show off in front of an audience, he will do a few flying changes. He forces his horse into a canter down the diagonal, yanking the horse's head and neck around at the transition point, and *voila*, a flying change. What often happens is aptly described in a sentence by Waldemar Seunig: "When the equestrian rabble starts to pay attention, art closes its eyes." (Seunig, W. 1960: *Reitergedanken am langen Zügel.* Heidenheim: Erich Hoffmann.)

The flying change at canter is a lesson for medium dressage and above. Before we can contemplate it, the horse must be able to canter from a walk on both reins confidently and above all he must be *straight.* In addition, he must have learned a simple change of lead on the center line while proceeding straight ahead—i.e., without depending on the wall — and he should not land on two tracks. Complete suppleness and strong forward impulsion are the other prerequisites. Finally, a flying change can only be practiced when the horse has mastered counter canter.

More nonsense is seen and heard regarding the flying change than any other aspect of riding. Here are three personal experiences to illustrate this:

1. For years a woman rider (who had owned her own horses for 20 years) had been dreaming of flying changes and upper level dressage. Although she had had eight horses (consecutively) in these 20 years, her riding ability was barely sufficient for the lowest level of dressage. Naturally, it was always the horse's fault that she made no progress. Finally, in order to make her dream come true, she purchased an older well-trained, advanced level horse for 40,000 DM. Still, she was not able to master the flying change. And worse yet, she wasn't even able to get this horse to canter correctly. I am sure she thought that, at the price she paid, upper level skills were automatically programmed into the horse.

2. A riding student who had had her own horse for six years and who had the previous summer begun to show in dressage with a good score in her first competition arrived one day at the riding school for a private lesson holding a double bridle and announcing, "Today I would like to begin with a flying change at a canter!" When I refused and told her that she wasn't even able to bring her horse to a canter from a walk, and had not yet mastered half-halts and other basic exercises, she was not gracious. She terminated her lessons with me.

Four weeks later she proudly informed me that her horse now executed flying changes. Another four weeks went by before she asked me to take her horse into training because it now jumped around continually and no longer had a decent canter.

3. Another rider with an insecure seat kept changing his horse's gait to a counter canter or a disunited canter after the second corner on the short wall. When I discussed the canter aids with him to help him eliminate the errors, he commented, "I don't understand; you see that my horse can make a flying change. That's upper level dressage. Don't make me out to be worse than I am." Then he told his riding colleagues that we were now practicing flying changes.

With these three examples I will leave the subject of every rider's pet fantasy.

What is lameness and what causes it?

Lameness is a result of pain. The horse wants to relieve the burden of a painful leg quickly and thus depends more on the healthy legs. In most cases lameness results from excessive demands. When they hear the words "excessive demands," most riders only think of jumping too high or long-distance riding, and that their horses have not been subjected to these activities. Instead they let their horses run around loose in the indoor arena, maybe let them jump freely once a week, and let them run wild in the paddock to let off steam, thinking that they are doing their horses a favor. They don't realize that these so-called treats are the basis for lameness and serious injury later on.

I will try, in a few broad strokes, to explain how these injuries develop. In training a young horse, the specific lessons—e.g., striking off at a canter, halting, rein back—should not be the main point, but rather the focus should be on gymnastics, developing muscles, and strengthening tendons, joints, and the circulatory system. The risk of demanding too much is especially great in the case of young horses because muscles, tendons and joints can be stressed only so far. Hoof problems and laminitis, so widespread today, are the result of subjecting youngsters to too much stress, particularly in jumping. But unforgivable mistakes are also made with older horses.

Here we should take some tips from sports medicine as it is applied to humans. Before a track and field athlete begins his actual exercises, he warms up his muscles with easy stretching. A warm muscle has a better supply of blood than a cold one, and can thus perform better. Muscles and tendons stand in a close relationship in the process of movement; the less trained a muscle is, the greater the strain on the tendon and the joint. Every rider should understand this and apply it to his or her horse.

Many riders who take very good care of their horses and love them very much like to let them run free in the indoor arena or romp energetically in the paddock. They like to see the horse's leaps and sudden stops and they even encourage them to wilder play. These same people will be astounded to learn that they are creating a basis for lameness that will appear later, because every leap and sudden stop can lead to torn tendons. With luck, only a few tendon fibers will tear and most damage will barely be noticeable. Nonetheless, these injuries often involve hyperextension and subsequent inflammation of the tendons. Lameness will eventually appear as the result of undue stress.

Riding over spongy terrain can also have very serious consequences. Anyone who has hiked through deep, soft sand dunes or who has hiked for hours at a time over spongy ground will know what this would demand of a horse. Trotting for half an hour on asphalt causes less damage to a horse's legs than fifteen minutes on a soft, yielding surface (although as a rule you should not trot for half an hour on asphalt). The cure for all tendon injuries is absolute rest and whatever else the veterinarian recommends.

Joint injuries also play a major role in lameness. The articular capsules of a horse become dry and inelastic as a result of standing in the stall. Synovial fluid is produced only after movement has begun and only then is the joint lubricated. According to the experts this lubrication process takes ten to twenty minutes. For this reason a horse coming directly from the stall must be ridden first at a walk and later at a loosening trot. Also, when longeing, there should be a sufficient period of work at a walk at the beginning. Anyone who canters or rides at a collected gait too soon after mounting should not be surprised at subsequent joint injuries.

These are the reasons for the rule that seems so rigid to many riders: "Every riding lesson starts at a walk with suppling exercises." Riders must finally realize that they should follow this rule, not as a favor to their riding instructors, but as a favor to their horses.

Riders should also know that joint injuries are not like tendon injuries, which are immediately noticeable because of inflammation. Joint injuries develop less obviously; by the time they are finally recognized, it is usually too late to cure them.

When longeing young and untrained horses, make sure that the horses canter on a large circle. When circles are too small, it is easy to demand too much from horses' legs. In fact, much damage is caused by inexpert longeing; many riders do not know how to longe. There is a mighty difference between longeing and having the horse run around in circles with a whip snapping behind him. You must learn how to longe; it is part of learning how to ride.

Many riders never suspect that they are riding their horses to injury by always riding with a crooked seat. The horse must adjust for this lopsidedness in his own balance, thereby causing stress to his joints. Stand in a corner on the long side of the arena and you will see that some riders always sit more to one side than the other and that this even causes the saddle to be crooked.

Often lameness can also be attributed to the hoof, but it is beyond the scope of this book to discuss hoof diseases in detail. A good blacksmith can often prevent hoof injuries from developing by supplying compensating orthopedic shoes.

Many riders spend too much time applying oils and ointments to their horses' hoofs; their attentions do more damage than good. The basic rule is to wash the hoofs regularly with water, especially the bottom of the hoof after picking it thoroughly clean. A stiff bristled brush is good for this. The glassy surface of the hoof should never be worked with hard objects. Small pebbles in the sole of the hoof and in the frog must be removed. After washing and drying the hoof, apply hoof dressing to the *sole* of the hoof once a week. The hoof should be oiled only *after* being washed and dried. Note that the oil should be rubbed into the hoof and not left as a thick layer on the surface. If the hoof is not growing well, massage the edge of the coronet with oil occasionally. The rules for hoof care generally conform to hydrotherapeutic recommendations for humans: riding through dew-drenched grass or hacking in a rain shower. The hoof needs moisture and exercise. After washing the hoof or riding through puddles and wet terrain, be sure to vigorously rub the fetlocks dry; if you don't, the horse can easily develop cracked heels.

7

The training schedule

One of the most interesting aspects of riding is keeping a written record of your horse's development and the headway made in training. Everyone who purchases a horse should start a notebook in which to record observations and thoughts. This way you can also check special situations for repeated occurrences, e.g., incidents of lameness, colic, the effect of weather conditions, or slackened performance when the winter coat is coming in.

I have kept a training log for most of the horses that I have been responsible for training. I find it interesting as well as enlightening to review the progress of the training with its high and low points, successes and failures. This facilitates decision making regarding correction and improvement.

I also prepare training records for my students with private horses. It is easier to check whether and what kind of progress a rider has made, or whether after three years his seat is as bad as it was on the day of the first entry in the log.

Horse's training log

Name: Gottfriedus
Born: 1975
Sire:. . . . . (Anglo-Arab)
Dam:. . . . . (Hannoverian)
Horse obtained from V. 4 years old, partially broken in.

March 1979

Horse appears to be psychologically overtaxed, training started too early and too hard! Very sensitive around the head, refuses to accept tight chin straps. Fearful, tight back, poor balance, practically green.

Initial training plan: Start from the beginning; longeing, trust, learning commands, praise and reprimand. Careful preparation for mounting the first time.

Middle of April

No problems with first mounting, walk with loose rein and rising trot with light contact through the whole arena, straight lines. Horse still sways, very sensitive mouth, at the slightest shortening of rein resists immediately by tossing the head and stepping into the rein.

May, June, July

Horse developing balance, initial resistance to the rein at trot, but then good progress. Good cadence at walk and trot, tires quickly and then overreaches.

End of July

Training plan for the next few weeks: Longeing.
Walk: initially with loose rein, later with very light contact. Rising trot with light contact, long neck, frame low. Ride straight! Ride forward!
　　Slight flexing of the lower jaw on the long side right and left, first at walk, then at trot: at walk develop a few strides of leg yielding.
　　Praise.
　　Practice half-halts, walk to halt, trot to walk, stand quietly after halting.
　　After finding balance on a straight line: Start circle work first at a walk, supple the inner side. If horse offers a canter, allow it; round off corners and help in the corners. No tempo change in trot yet. Don't expect too much.

Beginning of October

Training status: Horse stands correctly and quietly both during and after mounting.
　　Initial action: still somewhat tight.

Walk on a loose rein: flawless four-beat rhythm, supple, long neck, low frame. Walk on a long rein also good, horse moves into corners nicely.

Rising trot: light on the rein, rhythm and tempo good, harmonious, keen, well-balanced — alternating stretching and relaxing.

Bending work: bends willingly to the right; left is the difficult side.

Leg yielding: On the right a few good strides; left a start, but still unsatisfactory.

Halts: Accepts halts willingly with gentle rein; stands quietly after halting.

Work on circles at a walk: Horse keeps to the circle line, giving to the inside, allows itself to be guided on the soft inner side with the outside rein. Horse is content during all exercises, harmonious and keen. Starting to pivot on haunches.

Further training plan: Putting the horse on the aids dependably at trot and developing increased drive from the hindquarters.

Start circle work at a trot, exercises for the inside hind leg, leading rein with outside hand.

Perfect bending in serpentines across the arena.

Build on this carefully.

October 30

Strong forward movement at trot, but slight errors in rhythm on the long wall. Offers canter, moving nicely ahead. At the start only canter around the whole arena.

Horse offers a good seat, very keen, responds to back, leg, and hand aids: Everything in order.

Tires slightly after barely an hour of riding, so don't overdo it.

November 12

Introduce cavaletti: three rails at a walk, good. Riding out corners at trot getting good. Increasing and decreasing rectangles at walk, good start. Errors in rhythm at a trot disappear with light rein and guiding on outside rein. Still no tempo changes at trot since uneven rhythm appears then.

November 14

Minor injury to outside of left hock, minor swelling, nothing irregular.

November 20

First canter on the circle, very keen, the horse enjoys it!

December 10

Decreasing and increasing rectangles going well, first slight collection at a trot.

January 7, 1980

Beginning circle work by extending trot to canter. Horse cannot go a day without exercise, because the next day he is inattentive and too frisky.

March 7

Horse must be put under more energetic back and leg aids and fuller, more definite hand aids. Good progress at the trot, bending, nice bending of the whole spine. Trot nice and supple, hindquarters beginning to support more weight. He tenses up and bounces like a rubber ball. Canter still not up to snuff, still doesn't put enough weight on hindquarters.

April 2

Canter work improving, often offers incorrect canter on the right hand, try to improve seat and do more collection work before starting! Places weight on hindquarters well at a trot. Longer strides promising, but not enough.

April 28

All canter work improving, simple transition getting good.

May 28

Good canter on both leads, canter right good, in canter left he resists the flexion to the inside. First steps backward. Trotting good, but still irregular on the right.

June 7

Corrective shoes on forelegs. At the beginning dawdling, no spirit, no rhythm. Don't warm up too long, place weight on the hindquarters, then he moves well and is fun. Don't allow dawdling. Impulsion from hindquarters.

June 15

Uneven rhythm, front right no improvement. Veterinarian: Prolapsis of the coffin bone, alteration in the frog bone, hoofs too hard. Plan: A lot of moisture, wet grass, standing on turf, no longeing, a lot of riding straight, no tight circles, reduce weight on forequarters, corrective shoeing.

The first sixteen months of training described here already clearly show the connection between training difficulties and the changes in the right front hoof. This is a lesson that a horse should not be left standing too wet, nor too dry, especially when the horse spends little time outdoors. The hoof urgently needs the moisture that it absorbs from puddles, damp terrain, and wet grass.

8

Final reflections

The journey from a freshly broken youngster to a well-schooled dressage horse is a long one that requires a great deal of experience and endless patience on the trainer's part. There must be an overall training framework and short-term goals should be incorporated into the weekly plan. You can only focus on one thing at a time.

To avoid being misunderstood, I should say that a rigid and doctrinaire training plan must be avoided, rather follow the general framework recommended in this book, while allowing some flexibility. Good, solid groundwork based on exercise is important. We do not train horses simply to train horses, but as a means to an end. We want to preserve and cultivate the beauty of movement that is innate in a young horse. Often training entails far too much coercion and punishment. Many riders unload the frustrations they have collected during the course of the work day on their horses at night and then tell themselves that this falls under the rubric of training. This can go so far that the horse develops hives out of sheer nervousness when his rider appears in the evening. (In one case I know of, the horse had to get a tranquilizing suppository before it could be ridden.)

In many circles, deficient basic training of both rider and horse are evident. Often the path to the top is blocked by a young rider's delusions of stardom and unwillingness to work toward perfection. The achievements and reputation of German riders respected throughout the world are beginning to falter. Other countries, however, especially the United States, are discovering the secret of basic training from the "classical" school and are seeking experienced German trainers to bring to their country. Thus, in the United States in the past two or three years the level of performance has improved noticeably in comparison with other countries. The Olympic games in Los Angeles were an unmistakable indication of this.

Ironically, what riders in other countries are discovering as *new* training techniques are now being denigrated in Germany as old-fashioned. Except for a few official training institutions, there are few riding schools providing intensive basic training with instruction in longeing, small groups divided into young remounts and older remounts, lessons in theory, divisions according to performance level, and separate sections for curb bit instruction.

A young horse needs an understanding teacher, and we must make sure that it does not suffer physical or psychological damage during its training. If not overtaxed during training, horses can serve us until they are very advanced in age — occasionally even in equestrian competitions. There are many examples of this. But there are also examples of horses who have been poorly trained and whose health was ruined at a very early age. There is a fine line between conditioning and tearing down. A horse is a living creature — one of God's creations — not a piece of sports equipment. Many riders should contemplate this distinction.

The horse, like the classical art of riding itself, is a cultural treasure. It is possible that future generations will judge us according to how we have dealt with these treasures — whether we have demeaned them, or whether we have preserved them and passed them on. The horse serves humankind — and our obligation to him is also a cultural duty.

Bibliography

Becher, R. (1984) *Success with the Longe Line, Martingales and Bit.* 4th ed. Berlin and Hamburg: Paul Parey.

Büger, U. (1982) *Perfect Equitation.* 5th ed. Berlin and Hamburg: Paul Parey.

Deutsche Reiterliche Vereinigung [German Riding Association] *Guidelines for Riding and Driving,* Vols. I and II. Warendorf: FN-. Verlag.

Haugk, S. v. (1949) *The Equestrian ABC.* Hannover: Schaper.

Heiling, Dr. (1964) *The Perfect Horse.* 3rd ed. Frankfurt: DLG Verlag.

Klimke, R. *Cavalletti.* 6th ed. Stuttgart: Franckh'sche Verlagshandlung.

Knopfhart, A. (1987) *Evaluating and Selecting Riding Horses.* 4th ed. Berlin and Hamburg: Paul Parey.

Knopfhart, A. (1987) *Dressage from A to S.* 2nd ed. Berlin and Hamburg: Paul Parey.

Müseler, W. (1981) *Riding Primer.* 44th ed. Berlin and Hamburg: Paul Parey.

Paalman, A. (1986) *Jumping.* 6th ed. Stuttgart: Franckh'sche Verlagshandlung.

Podhajsky, A. (1965) *Classical Equitation.* Munich: Nymphenburger.

Riding Regulations (1912) HDv. No. 12. Berlin.

Seunig, W. (1960) *From Corral to Capriole.* 3rd ed. Zurich: Fretz & Wasmuth.

Seunig, W. (1965) *Equestrian Thoughts on a Long Rein*. Heidenheim: Erich Hoffmann.

Steinbrecht, G. (1978) *High School for Horses*. 10th ed. Aachen: Dr. R. Georgi.

Thiedemann, F. (1979) *The Jumper*. Edition Habervek.

Index